Collins

Good
Grammar

Collins

HarperCollins Publishers
Westerhill Road, Bishopbriggs, Glasgow G64 2QT

www.collins.co.uk

First published 2000 as Collins Wordpower Good Grammar

Second edition published 2004

Reissued with new cover 2005

Reprint 2

Cartoons by Hunt Emerson

ISBN 0 00 720867 7

A catalogue record for this book is available from the British Library

Typeset by Davidson Pre-Press Graphics Ltd, Glasgow G3

Printed and bound in Great Britain by Clays Ltd, St Ives plc

Contents

The Thirteen Gremlims of Grammar

1. Correct speling is essential.

2. Don't use no double negatives.

3. Verbs has got to agree with their subjects.

4. Don't write run-on sentences they are hard to read.

5. About them sentence fragments.

6. Don't use commas, that aren't necessary.

7. A preposition is not a good word to end a sentence with.

8. Remember to not ever split infinitives.

9. Writing carefully, dangling participles must be avoided.

10. Alway's use apostrophe's correctly.

11. Make each singular pronoun agree with their antecedents.

12. Join clauses good, like a conjunction should.

13. Proofread your writing to make sure you don't words out.

And, above all, avoid clichés like the plague.

GRAHAM KING (1930-1999)

Graham King was born in Adelaide on October 16, 1930.
He trained as a cartographer and draughtsman before joining
Rupert Murdoch's burgeoning media empire in the 1960s, where
he became one of Murdoch's leading marketing figures during the
hard-fought Australian newspaper circulation wars of that decade.
Graham King moved to London in 1969, where his marketing
strategy transformed the *Sun* newspaper into the United Kingdom's
bestselling tabloid; subsequently, after 1986, he successfully
promoted the reconstruction of *The Sunday Times* as a large
multi-section newspaper.

A poet, watercolourist, landscape gardener and book
collector, Graham King also wrote a biography of Zola, *Garden of
Zola* (1978) and several thrillers such as *Killtest* (1978). Other
works include the novel *The Pandora Valley* (1973), a semi-
autobiographical account of the hardships endured by the
Australian unemployed and their families set in the 1930s.

In the early 1990s, inspired by the unreadability and
impracticality of many of the guides to English usage in
bookshops, Graham King developed the concept of a series of
reference guides called The One-Hour Wordpower series:
accessible, friendly guides designed to guide the reader through
the maze of English usage. He later expanded and revised the texts
to create an innovative series of English usage guides that would
break new ground in their accessibility and usefulness. The new
range of reference books became the Collins Wordpower series,
the first four titles being published in March 2000, the second four
in May 2000. Graham King died in May 1999, shortly after
completing the Collins Wordpower series.

> *"The greatest and most necessary task remains, to attain a habit of expression, without which knowledge is of little use."*
>
> – Dr Samuel Johnson, LLD

Introduction: How to wrestle with grammar – and win!

It takes courage to pick up a book on grammar when schooldays are over. Real courage, if only distant (and probably unpleasant) memories survive of what the subject was all about.

But you have picked this one up. And take heart. Charlotte Bronte, author of *Jane Eyre* and one of the greatest exponents of the language, was hopeless in English at school. Her teachers complained that 'she knew nothing of grammar', and could read only 'tolerably' and write 'indifferently'.

More recently, millions of young people have been denied even basic instruction in how to write good English – victims of the quarter-century blackout when the fashionable view of the education establishment was that a knowledge of how the parts of speech work was unnecessary. The acquisition of language skills happened naturally, they preached.

And so it does, to a point. Learning and obeying all the rules of grammar won't automatically bestow excellence on your speech and writing; but completely ignoring them will almost certainly consign you to inarticulate semi-literacy.

Does being good at grammar help you in life? Thousands of people who hold down highly-paid top jobs can hardly spell or compose a coherent letter without help. Even *The Times*, regarded as a paragon of grammatical certitude, slips up with comforting regularity: 'According to the Adult Literacy and Basic Skills Unit,' it reported recently, 'one in four 16- to 20-year-olds have reading problems and more than one third have trouble with spelling.' (the first *have* should be *has*, to agree with its antecedent *one in four*). Embarrassingly, the slip-up occurred in an editorial on the need for the rigorous teaching of grammar.

Are we being picky, or what? The danger is, if we allow seemingly minor transgressions to go unnoticed, we could find ourselves grappling with a leaky language system reeking of confusion and ambiguity.

Surely computer technology can help us with grammar. It can go some of the way, yes, but over-reliance on corrective software can be dangerous. An English student, writing a character study of Bottom from *A Midsummer Night's Dream* for a drama exam, ran the essay through the word processor's grammatical check tool. Her sentence, 'Puck thought it would be fun to place an asses's head on Bottom' was highlighted with the instruction: *Avoid this offensive term. Consider revising.*

Just as it's considered necessary to accept some basic instruction before driving a car, pretty much the same applies to writing. Before driving a car you learn to recognise some of its more important parts: the ignition and lights, the steering wheel, clutch, gears, brake, petrol tank, windscreen wipers and so forth. It's also necessary to know just what each part does, and what happens when you press it, turn it, pull it or push it. You also need to learn some rules – about speed, signalling, red and green lights, traffic and road signs. When you do all this, you can drive. When you do it all well, you might even drive well. Of course many people learn to drive a car without professional instruction, but, insufficiently equipped, they are often a danger to themselves and others.

It's not too different with reading, speaking and writing. Yes, we get by. But learning or relearning the rules and principles that govern the use of the language can only improve our communication skills. And more than ever, effective communicating is vital to our lives, our success, our enjoyment.

By picking up this book you've recognised that to improve your communication skills you probably need to return to basics. You've picked up the right book. *Collins Good Grammar* is designed to explain, step by practical step, authoritatively but entertainingly, the workings of our language, and to help you wrestle with its grammar – and win!

What is Grammar?
Why use it?

This won't take long.

A language requires two elements to fulfil man's need to communicate effectively: a vocabulary and a grammar.

The vocabulary is the language's stock of words: combinations of symbols, signs or letters that have evolved to identify things and ideas. But words by themselves can never constitute a language. Imagine someone possessing all the words required to express the message in the first three sentences, but no method of putting them together to make sense. An attempt might look like this:

Grammar about what duration of the clock will not take much duration not take small duration reasons to tell.

It would be like trying to build a solid wall with tennis balls. What's needed is some cement or glue to stick them together, to create a structure that others will recognise. In the case of a language this glue is a system of rules called grammar.

Languages aren't created in a day; some have evolved over hundreds, even thousands of years, and are still evolving. The users of any language must constantly invent to adapt to fresh circumstances, and when invention flags they must borrow.

Not only words, but rules, too. English grammar contains rules that can be traced back to the Greeks and Romans: rules that helped the early users of our language to string their words together to create increasingly clearer and more complex messages. They enabled that meaningless jumble of words to take shape as a recognisable sentence:

> *To tell what grammar is and that grammar should be used*
> *will need not little time not long time but some little long time.*

A big improvement, but still clumsy and vague. Obviously the language still required some more words and rules. The speaker needed a word more precise than *tell*, such as *explain*. Also needed was a system for building phrases with their own meanings, and another system for adding inflections to basic words to indicate time and sequence: *explain, explaining, explained*. With such improvements the sentence not only becomes shorter but also expresses the speaker's intentions with greater accuracy:

> *Explaining what grammar is and why you should use*
> *grammar will not take a long time.*

Then users began to get clever by inventing idioms such as *not too long* to say in three words what it took nearly a dozen to say in an earlier version. They also learned about ellipsis. To avoid repetition they created pronouns to substitute for nouns, phrases and whole sentences. Here, *this* stands for the two questions:

What is Grammar? Why use it? This will not take long.

And then, finally, in the quest for even greater economy, the newly-invented apostrophe was brought into play, saving yet one more word:

What is Grammar? Why use it? This won't take long.

And, having recognised that the promise following the original question is now history – in the past – our grasp of grammar's immense potential allows us to write:

It hasn't taken long, has it?

None of this should really surprise you, because if you are a native user of English you are also an intuitive user of its grammar. Although you may have either never known or have forgotten the difference between a common noun and a proper noun; are a little uncertain about using semi-colons and possessive apostrophes; are sublimely unconscious of piling on clichés and couldn't recognise a split infinitive even if you were offered a fortune, you have always managed to be understood, to get your point across, to enjoy reading newspapers and magazines, to write letters and cards to your family and friends, to deal adequately with the demands of the workplace.

But ask yourself: am I cringing along in the slow lane, grammatically speaking, aware of the ever-increasing traffic in the faster lanes?

More than at any time in history, you are judged on your communication skills, whether in speech or in writing. The successful development of your personal life, your relationships and your career is now more and more dependent upon the way in which you express your thoughts, your insights, knowledge and desires into language. How well you accomplish this is just as dependent upon your understanding of grammar. In so many ways you are only as good as your grammar.

Few would dispute that this is the Age of Communication. Its message is that the media are expanding exponentially. You can respond to the challenges and demands, or you can allow it to pass you by.

By reading this far, you appear to have chosen the former course. That's courageous, and you should feel encouraged. If, however, you remain unsure or sceptical, proceed to the next section which should demonstrate to you that you probably know quite a bit more about grammar than you ever imagined.

And that will be a great start to mastering this essential and exciting skill.

You know more about grammar than you think

Yes, you really do know more about grammar than you think. You may not know what a prepositional complement is or what it does, and may never have heard of subordinator conjunctions or modal auxiliaries – and why on earth should you?

But from an early age you acquired a knowledge of grammar that saw you through your elementary and primary schooling. Whether your memories of what you were taught about grammar are fresh or distantly hazy, pleasant or mordantly painful, a surprising amount of grammatical know-how is parked somewhere in your memory. By reading and listening to others, you added to your knowledge and developed further grammatical skills. Thus you will find that this book will often merely explain and clarify what you already intuitively know about the principles and usage of grammar.

To prove this to yourself, try the following test, consisting of twenty examples of right and wrong use of the language. Record your answers by ticking the appropriate boxes. And here's a tip before you begin: although some grammar rules may seem hare-brained, most follow logical, commonsense principles.Rather than try to analyse the examples, try to 'listen' to what is being said.

1. One of these isn't a proper sentence. Which one is?

   A. *Any failure of the buyers to comply with the sale conditions, the damages are recoverable.*

   B. *Any failure of the buyers to comply with the sale conditions may result in damages being recovered.*

2. Here's another pair of sentences. One contains a fairly common mistake. Which one is correct?

   A. *On Sunday we heard the first chaffinch sing, we have several that come into our garden for crumbs.*

   B. *On Sunday we heard the first chaffinch sing; we have several that come into our garden for crumbs.*

3. There's something jarring in one of these sentences because in it there's an inconsistency. Which one is the correct sentence?

   A. *The Prime Minister, accompanied by several aides, were entertained by President Clinton at the White House.*

   B. *The Prime Minister, accompanied by several aides, was entertained by President Clinton at the White House.*

4. Oh, dear! There are some unwelcome and unnecessary marks in one of these statements. Which one is correct?

   A. *The three shops supplied all Jim's shirts and suits.*

   B. *The three shop's supplied all Jim's shirt's and suit's.*

5. Do you have an ear for good grammar? If you do you'll quickly spot the mistake. But which sentence looks and sounds right?

   A. *The public always expects us firemen to be at the scene of a fire within minutes.*

   B. *The public always expects we firemen to be at the scene of a fire within minutes.*

6. Although you may not know the difference between an adjective and an adverb you should easily pick the sentence that uses adverbs correctly.

   A. *Bert always drove real careful, and was proud of his record.*

   B. *Bert always drove really carefully, and was proud of his record.*

7. Many of us aren't sure about using *among* and *between*. Can you pick the correct usage?

   A. *The ice cream was shared among the three of them.*

   B. *The ice cream was shared between the three of them.*

8. Something weird is happening in one of these sentences. Which one avoids a rather bizarre atmospheric condition?

   A. *Tearing down the motorway at 80mph, the fog suddenly enveloped the car, forcing me to pull over.*

   B. *As I was tearing down the motorway at 80mph, the fog suddenly enveloped the car, forcing me to pull over.*

9. If you read these sentences carefully, you'll see that one doesn't make sense. Which one is clear and correct?

   A. *The judge remained both unimpressed by evidence and argument.*

   B. *The judge remained unimpressed by both evidence and argument.*

10. Don't get carried away by the racy prose; there's a fundamental error in one of these sentences. Which is the sentence without the error?

    A. *Then, as he lay silently beside her, she cried: A broken, hoarse cry that sprang from a buried memory of adolescence.*

    B. *Then, as he lay silently beside her, she cried: a broken, hoarse cry that sprang from a buried memory of adolescence.*

11. One sentence uses a word correctly; the other abuses it. Which is correct?

    A. *I gazed in wonder at the diamond, one of the most unique in the world.*

    B. *I gazed in wonder at the diamond, thought by many to be unique.*

12. In which sentence is the question mark used correctly?

    A. *Her mother was always asking? 'When are you going to get married'.*

    B. *Her mother was always asking, 'When are you going to get married?'*

13. Frank was confused in the following sentences, but do you get confused by *drink*, *drank* and *drunk*? Which is correct?

    A. *It was pretty obvious that Frank had drank rather too much.*

    B. *It was pretty obvious that Frank had drunk rather too much.*

14. One of these sentences contains a very common error – so common, in fact, that many now regard it as acceptable usage. But if you were a careful user of English, which sentence would you say was correct?

    A. *The teacher asked Judy to try and do better.*

    B. *The teacher asked Judy to try to do better.*

15. If you know the rule here, fine; but if not, your ear should tell you which sentence is grammatically correct. Well, which one?

    A. *Every man, woman and child is requested to assemble in the departure lounge.*

    B. *Every man, woman and child are requested to assemble in the departure lounge.*

16. Because it asks you to decide between *who* and *whom*, this question is one of the toughest in the test. But try, anyway, to pick the correct usage:

    A. *The Foreign Secretary, whom we are pleased to see is now fully recovered, will speak tonight.*

    B. *The Foreign Secretary, who we are pleased to see is now fully recovered, will speak tonight.*

17. Haven't had much to do with gerunds? Never mind – use your ear to choose the sentence which is strictly correct.

    A. *I hope she won't take exception to me calling in unannounced.*

    B. *I hope she won't take exception to my calling in unannounced.*

18. These sentences are worth thinking about. Which one do you think is correct?

    A. *A thousand visitors is not unusual on an average weekday.*

    B. *A thousand visitors are not unusual on an average weekday.*

19. If you listen carefully to what is being said here, one sentence will be quite clear in its meaning while the other could confuse you. Which is the unambiguous sentence?

    A. *After the game he talked at length to the captain and the manager.*

    B. *After the game he talked at length to the captain and manager.*

20. There are some discordant notes in one of these sentences. Which one is consistent and harmonious?

    A. *If one is to live happily among one's neighbours, you must learn to mind your own business.*

    B. *If you are to live happily among your neighbours, you must learn to mind your own business.*

If you are interested to know where you stand in your knowledge and use of English grammar, you should have attempted to answer all 20 questions. If you've made a guess at some of them, don't feel too guilty; some guesses will be right while others will be wrong.

Answers   Now turn to page 20 for the answers and explanations. The correct answers to questions considered to be more difficult receive more marks than those to easier questions.

Answers to the Grammar Test

1.   **B** is a proper sentence. **A** is not because it is incomplete, having no active verb, and makes no sense. See *Let's Look at Sentences*, page 25.

2.   **B** is correct. **A** is what is called a 'run-on' construction – two sentences spliced by a comma. The first sentence should have ended after *sing* and the second sentence begun with *We*. But as the two thoughts are related a better idea is to keep them in the same sentence and separated by a longer pause – a semi-colon. See *The Semi-colon*, page 164.

3.   **B** is correct. Although the PM was accompanied by several aides, we don't know whether they were entertained or not. However the sentence makes clear that President Clinton entertained the PM, singular, so the use of the singular *was* and not the plural *were* is correct. If sentence **A** read: '*The Prime Minister and several aides were entertained* . . . ' the use of *were* would be correct. See *Singular and Plural Nouns*, page 66.

4.   **A** is correct. The apostrophes in *shop's*, *shirt's* and *suit's* serve no grammatical purpose and are redundant. The apostrophe in *Jim's* is correct because it tells us that the shirts and suits are possessed by Jim.

5.   **A** is correct. *Us* is the objective form of the pronoun *we* and is used here to include the speaker and others – other firemen. *We* would be correct if the sentence were written *We firemen are expected by the public to be at the scene of a fire within minutes.*

6.   Sentence **B** is correct because it calls for the adverbs *really carefully* to describe how Bert drove. See *How adverbs work*, page 128.

7.   You share *between* two, or *among* three or more, so **A** is correct.

8.   The 'something weird' in sentence **A** is the bizarre spectacle of an 80mph fog tearing down the motorway (*Tearing down the motorway at 80mph, the fog*)! Sentence **A** contains what is known as a dangling or unattached participle, but **B** is quite correct. See *The Dangling, or Misplaced Participle*, page 109.

9.   Sentence **B** is clear and correct. If you study **A** closely you'll see that it makes no sense. The only way that *both* would work in that position would be in a sentence such as *The judge remained both unimpressed and bemused by the evidence and the argument.*

10.   A simple error but perhaps difficult to spot. In sentence **A** the colon after *cried* is followed by a capital *A*. A colon is not a full stop so what follows should not be capitalised. Sentence **B** is correct. See *The Colon*, page 168.

11.   The word *unique* means 'one of a kind', so it follows that you cannot have something or someone that is *most unique*, *quite unique* or *almost unique*. Either it is or it isn't. Sentence **B** is correct.

12.   **B** is correct. The question mark does not precede a question, it follows one.

13.　　**B** is correct. To indicate the correct sense of lapsed time the past perfect tense of the verb *drink* is called for: *had drunk*.

14.　　**B** is correct. While both *try and* and *try to* are generally considered to be acceptable, the careful user will regard *try and* as idiomatic and prefer the grammatically correct *try to* in sentence **B**. See *Prepositions*, page 141.

15.　　**A** is correct, because *every* refers to each individual. So regardless of how many men, women and children there are, the singular verb *is* is called for.

16.　　**B** is correct. In this case, apply the *he = who, him = whom* rule (see discussion of *who/whom* in the section on *Pronouns*, page 82). As the Foreign Secretary (*he*, the subject) is fully recovered, and will speak (the object), *who* is appropriate.

17.　　**B** is correct. Here, the pronoun *me* is converted to a verb which can be used like a noun and which can be possessive, hence *my calling*. See *Gerunds*, page 110.

18.　　**A** is strictly correct. Although *visitors* is plural, a *thousand visitors* here is short for 'to have a thousand visitors'. In other words the number of visitors has become a single unit (you could say, 'to have a big crowd') which requires a singular verb – *is* and not *are*. See *Singular and Plural Nouns*, page 66.

19.　　**A** is the unambiguous sentence because it makes clear that he talked to the captain *and* the manager – two people. **B** is unclear and could confuse, because he could have talked to the captain/manager – one person.

20.　　**B** is consistent and correct. The pronouns in sentence **A** lack concord: it begins with *one's* but then moves on to *you* and *your*. It would be correct if it were written as ' . . . **one** *must learn to mind* **one's** *own business*.'

Grammar Test Scorecard

Check your answers to the Grammar Test on pages 20-22
with the correct versions and explanations and enter the
results on the scorecard below. Award the appropriate
points for every correct answer.

Question	Score for correct answer	Your score
1	3	☐
2	2	☐
3	3	☐
4	1	☐
5	2	☐
6	2	☐
7	2	☐
8	3	☐
9	3	☐
10	2	☐
11	2	☐
12	1	☐
13	2	☐
14	2	☐
15	3	☐
16	4	☐
17	4	☐
18	4	☐
19	3	☐
20	2	☐
TOTAL	50	☐

Scores   The total score for all correct is 50.

If you score in the 25-50 range, you are among those who take considerable care over their speech and writing. Because you're aware of the pleasure and power that the effective use of the language can impart, you will almost certainly wish to continue to develop your knowledge of grammar and to renew acquaintance with its logic, its complexity, its beauty and its genius for contrariness.

If you score 20-25 you are certainly in the 'above average' category, which means that, grammatically speaking, you are halfway to becoming an extremely proficient writer and speaker.

For those of you who scored less than 20 – and please don't feel you are alone or part of a sub-literate minority – what follows in this book should be of special interest and value to you. You will never regret taking a few hours to polish your native know-how (even if it is a bit sparse or rusty) of English and its workings.

Let's Look at Sentences

Every time we speak we use sentences. They are the easiest of all grammatical units to recognise, so it seems sensible to begin with them.

Easy to recognise, yes, but hard to define. In his *Dictionary of Modern English Usage*, H W Fowler gives ten definitions by various grammarians, including:

- A group of words which makes sense.

- A word or set of words followed by a pause and revealing an intelligible purpose.

- A combination of words that contains at least one subject and one predicate.

- A combination of words that completes a thought.

None of these, however, exactly fills the bill, although it is difficult not to agree with the *Collins English Dictionary*'s definition:

'A sequence of words capable of standing alone to make an assertion, ask a question, or give a command, usually consisting of a subject and predicate containing a finite verb.'

More important is what sentences are for:

- To make statements

- To ask questions

- To request or demand action

- To express emotion

From a practical standpoint, a sentence should express a single idea, or thoughts related to that idea. It should say something. A popular rule of thumb is that a sentence should be complete in thought and complete in construction. And, from a practical point of view, you will soon find that certain rules must be observed if your sentences are to be clear, unambiguous, logical and interesting to the listener or reader.

That said, you still have plenty of scope to fashion sentences of almost any size and shape.

Here is a sentence: the opening sentence of Daniel Defoe's *The Life and Strange and Surprising Adventures of Robinson Crusoe* (1719).

> *I was born in the year 1632, in the city of York, of a good family, though not of that country, my father being a foreigner of Bremen, who settled first at Hull: he got a good estate by merchandise, and leaving off his trade, lived afterward at York, from whence he married my mother, whose relations were named Robinson, a very good family in that country, and from whom I was called Robinson Kreutznoer; but, by the usual corruption of words in England, we are now called, nay, we call ourselves, and write our name Crusoe, and so my companions always call me.*

Very few novelists today would have the nerve or the skill to begin a novel with a long sentence like that; for apart from its length it is also a skilfully wrought passage: clear, supple, flowing and ultimately riveting. If it were written today it would most likely appear as a paragraph of several sentences:

> *I was born in York in 1632, of a good family. My father came from Bremen and first settled at Hull, acquired his estate by trading merchandise, and then moved to York. There he met and married my mother, from a well established family in that county named Robinson. I was consequently named Robinson Kreutznoer, but in time my own name and that of our family was anglicised to Crusoe. That's what we're now called, that's how we write our name, and that's what my friends have always called me.*

Defoe's original is a fairly long sentence by any standards. Now try this sentence for size:

> *'But —— !'*

This one appears to defy everything we think we know about sentences, but it is a valid sentence just the same, as you will see when it is placed in its correct context:

> *Jane turned abruptly from the window and faced him with blazing eyes.*
> *'Well, you've finally done it! You realise we're all ruined, don't you? Don't you!'*
> *'But ——!' Harry was squirming. Speechless. He stepped back in an attempt to evade the next onslaught.*
> *It never came. Instead, weeping uncontrollably, Jane collapsed on to the settee.*

You can see that *'But —— !'*, short though it is, quite

adequately expresses a response and an action in the context of the middle paragraph (a paragraph can consist of one or more sentences with a common theme). Despite its seeming incompleteness, it is nevertheless a sentence of a kind, although some grammarians would label it a sentence fragment. Here are some more:

Her expression conveyed everything. Disaster. Ruin. Utter ruin.

Three of the four sentences here are sentence fragments. They're perfectly legitimate, but use them for emphasis only, and with care.

The long-winded sentence

Another kind of sentence, and one to avoid, is seen rather too often. Typically, it is rambling and unclear, usually the result of having too many ideas and unrelated thoughts jammed into it, like this one:

He said that the agreement would galvanise a new sense of opportunity and partnership between the countries and enable them to articulate the targets with regard to inflation, set by economically enlightened governments, which was always of great concern to every family in the European Union.

Would you really bother to try to unravel that sentence? No, life is too short, and that sentence is most likely destined to remain unread, its author's voice deservedly unheard. That's the price you pay for writing bad sentences. To demonstrate how the inclusion of irrelevant matter can cloud the intent and meaning of a sentence, consider this example:

Jonathan Yeats, whose family moved to the United States from Ireland in the late 1950s, and who later married a Mormon girl from Wisconsin, wrote the novel in less than three months.

We are bound to ask, what has the novelist's family to do with his writing a book in record time? Did the Mormon girl help him? Did his marriage inspire him to write like a demon? If not, why mention these facts? By the time we've reached the important part of the sentence – the fact that he wrote the book in less than three months – our attention has been ambushed by two extraneous thoughts.

American presidents are notorious for irrelevant rambling. The tradition began, apparently, with President Harding, of whom, when he died in 1923, a wit observed, 'The only man, woman or child who wrote a simple declarative sentence with seven grammatical errors is dead.' A sample:

> *I have the good intention to write you a letter ever since you left, but the pressure of things has prevented, speeches to prepare and deliver, and seeing people, make a very exacting penalty of trying to be in politics.*

But we must not grieve over Harding when we have former US president George Bush gamely carrying the national flag of gobbledegook:

> *I mean a child that doesn't have a parent to read to that child or that doesn't see that when the child is hurting to have a parent and help out or neither parent there enough to pick the kid up and dust him off and send him back into the game at school or whatever, that kid has a disadvantage.*

Well, enough of warnings. The point to remember is that although a sentence may be as long as a piece of string, long sentences may land you in trouble. A good sentence will be no longer than necessary, but this doesn't mean that you should chop all your sentences to a few words. That would be boring. To keep the reader alert and interested you need variety. If you examine this paragraph, for example, you'll find a sentence sequence that goes *short/long/long/short/medium/long/medium*. It's not meant to be a model, but it aims in the right direction.

When a sentence isn't a sentence

Here are some constructions that aren't regarded as 'proper' sentences:

> *Are unable to fill any order within 21 days.*
> *Date for the closing of.*
> *Thinking it an excellent opportunity.*

Clearly, there's something wrong with these. What is wrong is that these examples do not make sense. Nor are they in any context that would help them to make sense. They are incomplete because they are ungrammatical and do not express a thought or an action or carry any recognisable information. It has nothing to do with length, either; the following examples are extremely short but are grammatical and convey the intended information in such a way as to be unambiguous:

> *'Taxi!' ONE WAY Stop! Amount Due 'Damn!'*
> *'Leaving already?'*

Sentences are so versatile they can be confusing, so this might be a good time to take a closer look at the inner workings of the sentence. Despite the demonstration that even single-word 'sentences' can make sense, let's concentrate on what we might call a 'classic' sentence.

The inner workings of the classic sentence

Try to think of a sentence as a combination of two units:

The subject – What it is

The predicate – what we're saying about it

Here are some simple examples:

SUBJECT	PREDICATE
My	*word!*
Your book	*is over there.*
Dr Smith	*will see you tomorrow.*

The subject of a sentence does not have to precede the predicate. Every day we'll read hundreds of sentences in which the predicate precedes the subject:

PREDICATE	SUBJECT
It gradually became apparent that it was	*the odour of death.*
Over the horizon appeared	*an immense armada.*

Sometimes the subject of a sentence can be buried, or at least disguised. What are the subjects in these sentences?

A *How many more times must we do this long journey?*

B *You should see how my friend Jeremy deals with pushy salesmen.*

C *Take this load of rubbish to the shop for a refund.*

A is what is called an interrogative sentence which often transposes subject and predicate. If you think carefully about this example you'll probably conclude that the only possible candidate for the subject is *we* (**We** *must do this journey how many more times?*).

If you flushed out the subject in **A** you should have little trouble with example **B**, which is a similar construction. The subject here is *my friend Jeremy*.

Example **C** has what you could call a 'ghost' subject. It is an imperative sentence in which the subject is implied. What the sentence is really doing is commanding someone to undertake a task:

> *(Will you please) Take this load of rubbish to the shop for a refund.*

or   *(You) Take this load of rubbish to the shop for a refund.*

If you follow the logic of this you'll see that the subject here is *You*; the sentence itself is the predicate.

Quite often both the subject and predicate of a sentence can consist of two or more parts, or compounds:

SUBJECT	SUBJECT	PREDICATE
French and	*English literature*	*were not Amy's favourite subjects.*

SUBJECT	PREDICATE	PREDICATE
The three lads	*partied at night* and	*recovered by day.*

If you can digest all this you can put it at the back of your mind but you will find it a helpful guide in sentence construction. It will help you to know, for instance, that in a long sentence such as **James, my close friend and the grandson of the French artist Bernard Agate**, *is moving to New York*, that the portion in bold is the subject and *is moving to New York* is the predicate, while in **James** *is moving next month to the place he's always wanted to be – New York*, the single word *James* is the subject and the rest is the predicate.

The predicate can be a bit of a puzzle, mainly because it can consist of just a single verb or a number of elements that describe, modify or supply extra information. We make sense of this by recognising a **direct** and **indirect object**. In the sentence –

James is moving to New York.

– *James* is the subject and the rest is the predicate. The direct object of the predicate is *New York*. It isn't actually doing anything, but is having something done to *it*. If, however, the sentence expands a little –

James told me he was moving to New York.

– we now have not only a direct object (*New York*) but an indirect object – *me*.

Simple, Compound and Complex Sentences

Apart from the subject/predicate concept of sentences, there is another way of classifying these constructions. Single-word expressions such as 'Hey!', signs, catchphrases, greetings and so on, are called **irregular**, **fragmentary** or **minor sentences**. Sentences that are constructed to express a complete, independent thought are called **regular sentences**, and these are divided into **simple**, **compound** and **complex sentences**. These are worth exploring because in writing and speaking we use them all the time. Knowing about them should help us use them to better advantage.

A **simple sentence** consists of a single main clause:

We went to Bournemouth last week.
The storm brought down all the power lines.

A **compound sentence** consists of two or more main clauses, indicated in bold:

The storm brought down all the power lines *and*

caused havoc throughout Montreal.

Sam finally agreed to buy the car but still had doubts about the steering.

Both simple and compound sentences have one thing in common: neither have subordinate clauses (you'll find more on clauses on page 58). When you add one or more subordinate clauses to the sentence mix, you create a **complex sentence**. In these examples the main clauses are in bold and the subordinate clauses are in parenthesis:

The spacecraft (that caused the emergency) was considered obsolete.

She bolted through the door (which slammed behind her).

My grandfather has now retired, but the family business (that he started in 1928) is still going strong.

The last example, consisting of two main clauses and a subordinate clause, is really a **compound-complex sentence**, one of the most common sentence constructions.

From these examples you'll see that unlike simple sentences, compound and complex sentences express two or more thoughts. Let's take two simple sentences:

The money was spent on urban regeneration. The money provided hundreds of families with excellent houses.

Most of us, seeing this pair of sentences, would find it difficult to resist the urge to combine them:

The money was spent on urban regeneration and it provided hundreds of families with excellent houses.

Compound and complex sentences link connected thoughts in an economical way. Indeed, a third thought could safely be added:

The money was spent on urban regeneration and provided hundreds of families with excellent houses, but it did not take funds away from existing public housing schemes.

Beyond this you have to be careful, or risk confusing or overloading the reader. By the way, did you notice the two words used to link the three thoughts or sentences into one? They are *and* and *but*, conjunctions that are commonly used to build compound and complex sentences. (See discussion under *Grammatical Glue*, page 138.)

Types of Regular Sentences

Earlier, we defined four uses for sentences. Each of these calls for a different type of sentence, and it's worth knowing what they are:

- A **DECLARATIVE SENTENCE** makes a statement:
  A rose bush grew in the garden.
  Ben has just thrown a ball through the window.

- An **INTERROGATIVE SENTENCE** asks a question:
  Is that a rose bush in the garden?
  Did Ben just throw a ball through the window?

- An **IMPERATIVE SENTENCE** directs or commands:
  Look at that rose bush in the garden.
  See if Ben's thrown a ball through the window.

- An **EXCLAMATORY SENTENCE** expresses emotion:
  I wouldn't dream of touching that rose bush!
  I'll scream if Ben's thrown a ball through the window!

Another aspect of a sentence is that it can express thoughts or actions positively or negatively:

- *I like eating in restaurants* is a **positive sentence**.

- *I don't like eating in restaurants* is a **negative sentence**.

The difference may seem obvious in these two examples but a sentence can damage itself with the inclusion – sometimes unconsciously – of double negatives and near or quasi-negatives:

- ***I don't*** *know* ***nothing***. (non-standard double negative)

- *It was a* ***not unusual*** *sight to see the heron flying away.* (acceptable double negative)

- *I* ***hardly*** *saw* ***nobody*** *at the sale.* (negative and quasi-negative)
  There's ***no question*** *that Robert will pay the debt.* (negative, but the *no question* is intended to positively express 'no doubt whatsoever')

- *I* ***can't help but*** *applaud her generosity.* (intended to be positive but grammatically the sentence expresses a negative sense)

The second example is an instance of what is called **litotes** (pron. *LY-to-tees*), which is an elegant form of understatement expressed by denying something negative:

She's not a bad cook means *She's quite a good cook.*
The effect is by no means negligible means *The effect is quite noticeable.*

The negative/positive aspect of sentences is worth noting because a diet of too much negativism in your speech and writing can have an overall negative or depressing effect, and can be confusing, too. Sometimes it is better to express negative thoughts in a positive way. *She is not beautiful* or *She's by no means beautiful* are not only negative but vague – she could be statuesque or handsome. A more positive and precise description might be: *She is rather homely.*

The 'Voice' of a Sentence

All sentences are either **active** or **passive**, and it is up to the user to decide which 'voice' to use. This voice is not something you hear, by the way; it is rather a point of view. The voice of a sentence is the kind of verbal inflection used to express whether the subject *acts* (active voice) or is *acted upon* (passive voice). Here are a few examples of both:

● **ACTIVE**   *The favourite won the 3.30 hurdle event.*
              Her boyfriend bought the ring.
              Very few can appreciate his paintings.

● **PASSIVE**   *The 3.30 hurdle event was won by the favourite.*
              The ring was bought by her boyfriend.
              His paintings can be appreciated by very few.

Even a cursory glance at these sentences tell you that active sentences are more direct, lively and interesting than passive sentences, which tend to be detached and impersonal – ancient history, as some would have it. Generally, we use the active voice almost exclusively in our everyday speech and writing, while the passive voice is reserved mostly for technical, scientific and academic writing.

Being aware of the roles of active and passive voice in sentences helps to avoid mixing them – a topic discussed a little later (see *Harmony in the Sentence*, page 41).

The Mood of a Sentence

Another quality of a sentence is its 'mood', or more accurately the mood of its verb – another kind of verbal inflection used to express the speaker's intention in a sentence, such as making a statement (**indicative**), giving a command (**imperative**), or posing a hypothetical situation (**subjunctive**). Here are some examples:

- **INDICATIVE MOOD** *She's tired and exhausted.*
  Summer is just around the corner.
  Is that all we're having for dinner tonight?

- **IMPERATIVE MOOD** *Call me tomorrow.*
  Don't call me, I'll call you.
  Tell me about it tomorrow.

- **SUBJUNCTIVE MOOD** *If I were you, I'd tell them about it.*
  The judge ordered that he be tried for theft.
  The poor girl wished she were dead.

Although we often use the subjunctive mood without being aware of it (*I wish you were here*; *God Save the Queen*; *So be it*; *If I were you I'd . . .*) perhaps because such utterances are idiomatic, it is nevertheless the mood that gives us the most trouble.

Here is a sentence from the *Guardian* which, if it *were* grammatically correct (note the subjunctive *were*, indicating an imagined or possible situation), would have been expressed in the subjunctive mood:

Incorrect *No wonder the Tory Party turned him down as a possible candidate, suggesting he **went away** and **came back** with a better public image.*

Correct *No wonder the Tory Party turned him down as a possible*

*candidate, suggesting he **go away** and **come back** with
a better public image.*

Let's face it – most of us would avoid such a construction
where the correct use of the subjunctive mood requires grammatical
know-how of a very high order. On the other hand we might have
the wit to insert *should* before the verb *go away*, rendering the
sentence both grammatically correct and more readable:

*No wonder the Tory Party turned him down as a possible
candidate, suggesting that he should go away and come back
with a better public image.*

The correct use of the subjunctive can undoubtedly look
strange, as in this example quoted by Eric Partridge in his *Usage
and Abusage*: *Although he die now, his name will live.* Not surprisingly
most writers tend to avoid or ignore the subjunctive, so that
sentences such as *I insist that he is sacked (I insist that he **be** sacked)*
and *It is to be hoped that she stops her bad behaviour (It is to be hoped that
she **stop** her bad behaviour)* are now considered acceptable. This may
be so, but careful and elegant writers will always fall back on the
subjunctive mood to express hypothetical situations in sentences
usually containing *if* and *that (If she were here, I would tell her about
Tom; I suggest that she be told immediately.)*

Ellipsis: Trimming away 'Sentence Fat'

Nobody these days wants to write more words than necessary,
or to be forced to read fifty words when the information could have
been conveyed with half that number. We have already seen that
by combining simple sentences into compound and complex
sentences we can economise on words and even enhance clarity; but
there is another grammatical convention that allows us to trim away
words we don't need. It's called **ellipsis** and it works like this:

WITHOUT ELLIPSIS	*When the children were called to the dinner table they came to the dinner table immediately. Harry Green had more coins in his collection than Thomas had coins in his collection.*
WITH ELLIPSIS	*When the children were called to the dinner table they came immediately. Harry Green had more coins in his collection than Thomas had in his.*

The reason we can get away with omitting part of the structure of sentences is that, if the listener or reader is paying attention, he or she will automatically supply the missing words from the context of what is being said or written. There is no loss of clarity, either; on the contrary, repetitive words can lead to boredom.

We resort to ellipsis constantly in our everyday communicating:

Leaving already?	means	*(Are you) leaving already?*
See you!	means	*(I will) see you (later, tomorrow, etc)*
Coming?	means	*(Are you) coming (with me)?*

Sometimes our economising extends to dropping what were once considered essential words:

He was unceremoniously kicked out the door.
The hat Rita bought is a total disaster.

If we heard these sentences spoken in an informal context we would hardly regard them as ungrammatical as, nowadays, even the strictly grammatical versions look a little odd to our eyes:

*He was unceremoniously kicked out **of** the door.*
*The hat **that** Rita bought is a total disaster.*

Such sentences are considered informal, although their meanings are perfectly clear. If a hostess greets a guest with, 'I am delighted that you could come', isn't she being a trifle formal? More likely, the greeting would be, 'I'm delighted you could come!'.

Although omitting *that* in sentences may now be acceptable, remember that it can sometimes lead to ambiguity. At the other extreme is the multiple *that*: *He pointed out that that that in the sentence was superfluous.* What can you do about *that*?

Harmony in the Sentence

What if Shakespeare had written in *Hamlet: To be, or not being – that is the question?* Well, of course he didn't, and wouldn't. From time to time scholars have pointed out examples of the Bard's bad grammar but sentences with faulty harmony in his plays would be hard to find.

Perhaps the most important principle in the construction of sentences is what is called **harmony** – or concord, consistency or parallelism – meaning that all the units in a sentence must agree and harmonise with each other. We can spot most inharmonious constructions, because they usually jar:

> *February is usually a succession of rain, hail and snowing.*

That sentence mixes two nouns and a participle, and it screams out at you, doesn't it? An harmonious construction would prefer to group three nouns:

> *February is usually a succession of rain, hail and snow.*

Alternatively, we could use a trio of participles to achieve harmony:

> *In February, it is usually either raining, hailing or snowing.*

41

Phrases in a sentence should match, too. In this example the second phrase is out of harmony with the first:

> **Bad grammar** is like **having bad breath** – even your best friends won't tell you.

There are two easy ways to remove the discord here. One is to match the phrase *bad grammar* with a similar adjective/noun phrase; the other is to add a parallel participle to *bad grammar* to match *having bad breath*:

> **Bad grammar** is like **bad breath** – even your best friends won't tell you.
>
> **Using bad grammar** is like **having bad breath** – even your best friends won't tell you.

Misplaced conjunctions (joiners) are another source of discord in sentences. Perhaps the two most common offenders are *either/or* and *not only/but also*:

CONFUSING   *They had to agree **either** to visit the museum **or** the gallery.*

*The house was **not only** affected with woodworm **but also** by years of neglect.*

CORRECT   *They had to agree to visit **either** the museum **or** the gallery.*

*The house was affected **not only** by woodworm **but also** by years of neglect.*

Another form of discord is the shift from active to passive voice in a sentence, or vice versa:

My father painted those pictures, which he left to me.

That sentence switches from **active** (*My father painted those pictures*) to **passive** voice (*which he left to me*). To achieve harmony, keep to the same voice:

ACTIVE   *My father painted those pictures, and left them to me.*

PASSIVE   *Those pictures were painted by my father, which he left to me.*

Clearly, the sentence that uses the active voice is the easier to read. A similar sort of discord is created when a sentence mixes personal and impersonal points of view:

> *The **student** should always exercise care and judgement because **you** will never succeed with slipshod thinking.*
>
> ***One** should always exercise care and judgement because **you** will never succeed with slipshod thinking.*

In the first example, consistency in person can be achieved by replacing *you* with *he or she*; in the second, the writer should either stick to the generic pronoun *one* throughout the sentence, or change the opening *One* to *You*.

Although perhaps not causing discord, faulty word order or misplaced modifiers in sentences can create confusion and chaos in otherwise simple sentences:

> *I saw you in my underwear!*

could mean either *I saw you when I was wearing only my underwear* or, more ominously, *I saw you, wearing my underwear!* Such a sentence could create not only confusion, but a most alarming scene. The misplaced modifier has been responsible for some hilariously ambiguous sentences:

> *Last night Helen went to see Elton John in a new dress.*
> *We have a parrot in a cage that talks.*

43

We can fit you in a new swimsuit that flatters – right over the phone!

You see very few signposts rambling around Wales.

The bomb was discovered by a security man in a plastic bag.

Send us your ideas on growing dwarf roses on a postcard.

However, of all the factors that can result in inharmonious sentences, the most prevalent is probably disagreement between the verb with its subject. In other words, a singular subject requires the singular form of a verb, and a plural subject requires the plural form of a verb: *this book, these books; that book, those books; she sings, they sing*. The following sentences ignore this:

*We **was** furious at the umpire's crazy decision.*

*Fifteen **paintings was** sold at auction last week.*

They should, of course, read:

*We **were** furious at the umpire's crazy decision.*

*Fifteen **paintings were** sold at auction last week.*

But look what happens when we 'collectivise' the subjects:

*The **team was** furious at the umpire's crazy decision.*

*A **collection** of paintings **was** sold at auction last week.*

Because we've gathered the players together into a team, and combined the paintings into a collection – that is, into single groups – we're back to using singular verbs. The important thing is to keep subjects and verbs in agreement in a sentence. While most of us would regard these examples as obviously faulty, many of us might stumble when confronted by nouns and noun phrases that can take either singular or plural forms. Nouns such as *team, family* and *committee* can be treated as singular or plural depending upon the context in which they are used. This is discussed at some

44

length in *Singular and Plural Nouns*, page 69, but meanwhile here is an example of how carelessness with verb and subject agreement can cause bewilderment and ambiguity.

The noun, in this case, is a name: the Human Fertilisation and Embryology Authority. What follows is from an article in *The Times* (22/11/96 – 'Widow Barred From Taking Husband's Sperm Abroad') which is an extraordinary cocktail of inconsistencies:

> *She was told by the Human Fertilisation and Embryology Authority that **they** would review her case . . . Diane Blood is outraged at the way the Authority has behaved . . The Authority **have** not even given any of **their** reasons . . the Authority said **it** would review the issue . . and **it** would not use **its** discretionary powers . . but said **they** wanted to 'leave no stone unturned' in **their** review and would give **its** reasons . . .*

That passage is a sobering lesson on the importance of, first, deciding whether your noun is singular or plural, and then sticking with the decision!

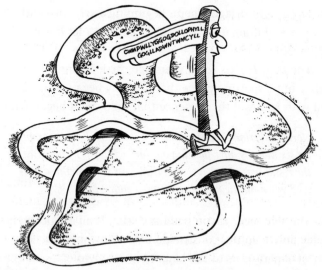

SENTENCES – You see very few signposts wandering around Wales . . .

Starting a Sentence with 'And' and 'But'

One of the more persistent grammatical superstitions is that you can't begin a sentence with conjunctions such as *And* and *But*. This is curious, because many of the finest writers in the English language – Shakespeare, Blake, Tennyson, Kipling, to name just four – have kicked off sentences with *And*, and so has the Bible: read the opening chapter. Probably the most popular rebel was Blake, who chose to begin his poem (better known as *Jerusalem*) with 'And did those feet in ancient time . . . '

Much the same applies to *But*. This time Thomas Macaulay, in his *The History of England*, is the hero of the rebel cause:

> *There were gentlemen and there were seamen in the navy of Charles the Second. But the seamen were not gentlemen; and the gentlemen were not seamen.*

There is no rule to say that you can't begin a sentence or a paragraph with the conjunction *But*. When you want to express a doubt or outright disagreement, beginning a sentence with *But* can emphasise and dramatise your point. *But* don't let it become a sloppy habit!

The *Daily Express* some years ago carried a memorable sentence in its sporting pages that not only began with *But*, but ended with *but*. And the sentence that followed it began with *And*:

> *Northumberland and Humberside will each hold the trophy for six months after fighting out an exciting 1-1 draw. But if the result was indecisive, then the soccer was anything but. And when all the medals have been engraved . . .*

The sentence, as you will have seen, is all at once a simple, complex and beautiful construction. As Winston Churchill, one of the most expert users of the language, once wrote: ' . . . I got into my bones the essential structure of the ordinary British sentence –

which is a noble thing'. Before we pass on to how a sentence is actually assembled with different kinds of words, it's worth remembering the hierarchy in which it exists:

A **word** consists of one or more morphemes (speech elements).

A **phrase** consists of one or more words.

A **clause** consists of one or more phrases.

A **sentence** consists of one or more clauses.

A **paragraph** consists of one or more sentences.

Same word – different roles

We all know what the word round means – or do we?
Here it is, in five different roles. Can you tell where it is used
as a noun, preposition, adjective, verb and adverb?

A   *The people gathered **round**.*

B   *I bought a **round** of drinks.*

C   *You **round** your lips when speaking.*

D   *He has a **round** face.*

E   *We drove **round** France last week.*

(A *adverb*; B *noun*; C *verb*; D *adjective*; E *preposition*)

The Building Blocks of Sentences: Parts of Speech

In Victorian times, when life was simpler, so, apparently was grammar. Here is a little verse widely used to teach young children the parts of speech during the latter part of the 19th century:

Three little words we often see,
Determiners, like *a*, *an* and *the*.

A ***Noun's*** the name of anything,
A *school* or *garden*, *hoop* or *string*.

An ***Adjective*** tells the kind of noun,
Like *great*, *small*, *pretty*, *white* or *brown*.

Instead of nouns the ***Pronouns*** stand –
John's head, *his* face, *my* arm, *your* hand.

Verbs tell of something being done,
To *read*, *write*, *count*, *sing*, *jump* or *run*.

How things are done, the ***Adverbs*** tell,
Like *slowly*, *quickly*, *ill* or *well*.

A ***Preposition*** stands before
A noun, as *in* a room, or *through* a door.

Conjunctions join the nouns together,
Like boy *or* girl, wind *and* weather.

The ***Interjection*** shows surprise,
Like *Oh*! How charming. *Ah*! How wise!

The whole are called 'Nine Parts of Speech',
Which reading, writing and speaking teach.

For millions of Victorian children this rhyme served as a gentle introduction to the terrors of **parsing** – the art of analysing the various roles played by words in a sentence. Whether the terror was real or imagined no doubt depended upon how the subject was taught. For the majority of children it was probably never an easy business to grasp, and this went for the teachers, too, to the extent that for a quarter of a century from the 1960s it was the misguided fashion in many quarters not to teach it at all. As a result many millions of today's adults in the English-speaking world have a big black hole in their grammatical education.

The fact that many words defy a single classification doesn't make things easier. We have seen how the word *round* can play five different roles depending upon how it is used in a sentence. Many other words are similarly versatile: *love* can act as a noun, verb and adjective, and so can *light*; *fast* can play the roles of noun, verb, adjective and adverb, and so on. *That* can be used as an adjective and as a pronoun:

> **That** *jacket belongs to me.* (adjective)
> **That** *is my jacket.* (pronoun)

Words – especially **neologisms**, or newly-coined words – also have the confusing habit of migrating from one class to another:

> *The doctor observed the patient's* **knee jerk**. (noun / verb)
> *His speech produced the inevitable* **knee-jerk** *reaction.*
> (adjective)
> *The President was a master of the art of the* **knee-jerk**. (noun)

Not all words have this chameleon quality, however. All words can be divided into two broad classes: **open classes** (which freely admit new words) and **closed classes** (which rarely do). For example:

OPEN CLASSES

Nouns	*software, gazumper, Fergy, tummytuck, spin doctor*
Adjectives	*neural, digital, cellular, quaffable, hands-on*

Verbs	*outed, overdosed, stargaze, deselect, nuke*
Adverbs	*breezily, chaotically, totally, tackily*
Interjections	*Phew! aahhh, ouch! Phooorrh!*

CLOSED CLASSES

Determiners	*the, which, my, that, your, these*
Pronouns	*I, me, we, hers, someone, whom*
Conjunctions	*and, or, but, when, since, as*
Prepositions	*at, with, in, by, to, from*
Auxiliaries	*be, may, can, will, were, must*

You can see from these examples that the closed classes of words are more or less static; it is very difficult to create new determiners or substitutes for *the*, *my* and *your*. The open classes, however, are expanding all the time.

At this point a pause may be useful, because you are being confronted with grammatical terms which may mean little or nothing to you. But to make sense of grammar it is impossible to avoid familiarity with at least a handful of basic terms. These will, however, be kept to a workable and untaxing minimum.

Let's begin with the 'parts of speech' – the components or building blocks of human communication. While you may not recognise the terms nor fully appreciate the roles they play, you are using them almost every minute of the day in your speech and writing. A simple analysis of a sentence might look like this:

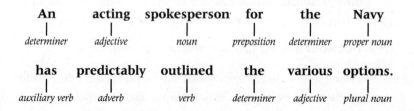

If you're ever in doubt about the grammatical status of any word, a good dictionary will tell you. Apart from defining a word's meaning the entry will also identify its use as a noun (*n*), adjective (*adj*), adverb (*adv*) etc, and often give examples of usage.

What follows now is a brief outline of each of the nine classes into which all words are grouped according to their function. This is designed to help you find your feet on the nursery slopes of the grammatical piste. A more detailed discussion on each word class follows.

Nouns

A **noun** is a name – of a place, an object, a person, an animal, a concept, of anything:

PLACES	*street, home, Germany, Paris, heaven*
OBJECTS	*plate, chair, tree, chamber pot, air*
PERSONS	*Einstein, Michael Jackson, Caroline*
ANIMALS	*pony, pig, wolfhound, chimpanzee*
CONCEPTS	*option, bad temper, ability, direction*

We also recognise types of nouns. All nouns are either **proper nouns** – that is, names that are specific or unique:

Marilyn Monroe, Saturday, The Rake's Progress, Mercedes, Brooklyn Bridge, Easter

or **common nouns**, which describe groups or members of groups, rather than individuals, or which broadly identify something:

boy, motor cars, tea, hair, darkness, opinions, anger, idea

You'll notice that proper nouns start with capital letters, and that common nouns don't. Common nouns are also divided into

concrete and **abstract** nouns, **count** and **non-count** nouns, **singular**, **plural** and **collective** nouns, and these are all discussed in *Naming Things: Nouns*, on page 64.

Verbs

Verbs are all about doing and being. They're action words. They're the engines that drive sentences to make them do something. Imagine trying to get through a day without these workhorses:

wake, woke, eat, drink, walked, drove, go, talked, do, keep, appear, exist, become, sleeps, dream

You can see, even from these few examples, that verbs take several forms, some ending in *-s*, *-ed*, and so on, and in fact most verbs have four or more forms to help us grasp when an action is taking place:

eat, eats, eating, eaten, ate
write, writes, writing, wrote, written

If you look up the words *eats*, *eating*, *eaten* or *ate* in a dictionary you may have difficulty finding them. However you *will* find them in the entry following the basic verb *eat*, which is called the **headword**, along with derivatives such as *eatable*, *eater*, *eating house*, *eatables*, *eat out*, *eat up*, *eat one's heart out*, etc.

Apart from their multiplicity of forms, verbs are notoriously variable: they can be **regular** (where they follow certain rules) and **irregular** (where they don't); they can be **main** verbs or **auxiliary** verbs, **transitive** and **intransitive**, **finite** and **infinite**. But don't let these grammatical gremlins scare you because they will be exposed for the poor, simple workaholics they are in the section on verbs on page 95.

Adjectives

Life without **adjectives** would be difficult, frustrating and extremely dull, because adjectives describe and modify things:

> *hot, freezing, beautiful, hairy, user-friendly, brainless, distasteful, pathogenic, pliable*

Some adjectives give themselves away by their endings: *-ing*, *-y*, *-less*, *-ful*, *-ic* and so on. They can also end with *-ly* which can cause us to confuse them with adverbs, which often end with the same suffix.

Simply put, adjectives add something to nouns and pronouns by modifying –

> *It was a **dreary** match.*
> *We made a **late** start.*

or by extending or reinforcing a noun's descriptive power –

> *It was an **obvious** mistake.*
> *The lady possessed **hypnotic** charm.*

You'll see that all the adjectives in the examples so far have come before the noun, but this need not always be the case:

> *The lady's charm was **hypnotic**.*

There is a fuller discussion of adjectives and how to use them on page 120.

Adverbs

Because they add information, **adverbs** are close relations to adjectives, as you can see:

Adjectives	**Adverbs**
essential	*essentially*
hypnotic	*hypnotically*
interesting	*interestingly*
dark	*darkly*

Don't be tricked, however, by believing that all adverbs end in *-ly*. They're very common, but the adverb family includes several other forms: *afterwards, enough, always, nevertheless, otherwise*.

The difference between adjectives and adverbs is that **adjectives** modify **nouns** and **pronouns**, while **adverbs** describe or modify **verbs**, **adjectives** and even other **adverbs**:

MODIFYING A VERB *He **trudged wearily** along the road.* (How did he walk along the road?)

MODIFYING AN ADJECTIVE *She's an **exceedingly lucky** girl.* (To what extent is she lucky?)

MODIFYING ANOTHER ADVERB *The engine turned over **very smoothly**.* (How smoothly did it turn over?)

Adverbs are often required where adjectives are incorrectly used, and vice versa. A guide to their usage will be found on page 120.

Pronouns

Pronouns are stand-ins for nouns and noun phrases, and are especially useful for avoiding repetition:

WITHOUT A PRONOUN *He saw James in the bar, and went over to meet James.*

Was I aware that Marcia was married?
Of course I knew Marcia was married.

WITH A PRONOUN
He saw James in the bar, and went over
*to meet **him**.*
Was I aware that Marcia was married.
*Of course I knew **she** was.*

You can readily see that pronouns are indispensable, and *they* (pronoun) form a major part of *our* (pronoun) everyday speech.

We divide pronouns into **personal pronouns** (*I, me, you, he, she, it*), **possessive pronouns** (*mine, ours, his, theirs*), **reflexive pronouns** (*myself, themselves*), **demonstrative pronouns** (*this, these, those*), **interrogative pronouns** (*who? what? which?*), **relative pronouns** (*who, whom, which, that*), **indefinite pronouns** (*all, any, many, everyone, few, most*) and **reciprocal pronouns** (*one another, each other*).

If you experienced a slight prickly sensation when glancing through those definitions the reason is most likely that pronouns can create more grammatical havoc than any other class of words. But when you've studied the detailed section on pronouns on page 77 you'll feel much more at home with these useful surrogate nouns.

Determiners

Determiners precede nouns and noun phrases, and the best known and most common of them are:

- *the* – known as the **definite article**, and

- *a* and *an* – known as **indefinite articles**

It's easy to see why they are described so; *the* is always specific, referring to a definite thing, person or entity, while *a* and *an* are used to refer to singular count nouns:

- ● *the* house over there; *the* woman in the red dress; *the* Hippodrome

- ● *a* large house; *an* angry young man; *a* good party; *an* eel pie

Words functioning as determiners – adjectives and pronouns, for example – exist in great variety, and help us to indicate quantity (*some* wine); ask questions (*whose* wine?); denote possession (*my* wine), and express emotion (*what* wine!). Numbers can function as determiners, too: *a thousand* thanks! *first* race, *half* a minute. Get the full story on determiners on page 139.

Conjunctions

Think of **conjunctions** as link-words that join two nouns, phrases, clauses or parts of a sentence:

*She asked Bernard if he intended going out **and** he told her to mind her own business.*
*She told him he could stay **if** he promised to be more polite.*

There are three types of conjunctions: **coordinating conjunctions**, which link words, phrases and clauses of equal importance; **subordinating conjunctions**, which link less important units to one or more of greater importance; and **correlative conjunctions**, which are used in pairs. They are all described on page 141.

Prepositions

While conjunctions link in a fairly straightforward way, **prepositions** link by relating **verbs** to **nouns, pronouns** and **noun phrases**. In particular they unite two sentence elements in such a way as to provide extra information about space, time, and reason:

*Judith travelled to New York **in** a 747 and flew **through** a storm.*

*Lawrence went down to the beach **at** noon.*

*Lizzie went to the arcade **for** a new swimsuit.*

We use prepositions constantly (try getting through a day without using *as*, *by*, *in*, *on*, *to* and *up*, to name just a few!) and misuse them occasionally. Should you, for example, end a sentence with a preposition? The answer, and more about this interesting member of the grammatical glue family, will be found on page 146.

Interjections

Interjections and **exclamations** are self-explanatory:

Wow! Hey! Shhhh! Blimey! Oh! Cheers!

Although these examples, expressing surprise, excitement or some other emotion, are followed by exclamation marks, these are not always necessary:

Okay, *let's get it over with.* **Ah-ha***, that's better.* **Mmmm** . . .

For further insight into interjections, see page 152.

Phrases and Clauses

We've now surveyed the different classes of words we use to construct sentences. However we should, at this point, also familiarise ourselves with two units or groups of words that are usually found in sentences: **phrases** and **clauses**.

A **phrase** is a group of words working as a unit but unable to stand alone or to make sense, but the definition can also include single words. The logic of this is demonstrated when we shrink a conventional phrase:

*I love **that dry white wine from Australia**.*

*I love **that dry white wine**.*

*I love **that white wine**.*

*I love **that wine**.*

*I love **wine**.*

The sets of words in bold are all phrases. The key word *wine* is called the headword, and because it is a noun, all five phrases are called **noun phrases**.

There are five kinds of phrases, each named after the class of the headword:

NOUN PHRASE	*They loved **their first home**. (home* is a noun)
VERB PHRASE	*We **have been burgled**. (burgled* is a verb)
ADVERB PHRASE	*Come **through the doorway**. (through* is an adverb)
ADJECTIVE PHRASE	*It's too **difficult to do**. (difficult* is an adjective)
PREPOSITIONAL PHRASE	*They walked **along the path**. (along* is the introducing preposition; *the path* is a noun phrase)

In the previous chapter we described three kinds of sentence: the **simple sentence**, consisting of a single main clause; the **compound sentence**, consisting of two or more main clauses, and the **complex sentence**, consisting of a main clause and one or more subordinate clauses. Fine – but what, exactly, are clauses?

A **clause**, quite simply, is a unit of related words which contains a subject and other words, always including a verb, which give us information about the subject:

The patient stopped breathing, so I shouted for the nurse.

In this example, *The patient stopped breathing* is a **main clause** of the sentence, because it can stand alone. In fact, if you put a full stop after *breathing* it becomes a legitimate sentence. But *I shouted for the nurse* is also a main clause because it can stand alone, too. What we have is a **compound sentence** consisting of two main clauses coordinated by the adverb *so* – here used as a conjunction:

main clause	*coordinator*	*main clause*
The patient stopped breathing	*so*	*I shouted for the nurse.*

Now let's construct a sentence in a different way – this time with a main clause and a subordinate clause:

This is the patient who stopped breathing.

You can pick the main clause because it can stand on its own: *This is the patient*. The rest of the sentence consists of *who stopped breathing*, which is the **subordinate clause** because it can't stand on its own:

main clause	*subordinate clause*
This is the patient	*who stopped breathing.*

You can add more information to a subordinate clause, but regardless of how much extra information you pile on it remains a subordinate clause because it is always subordinate to the main clause, serving only to influence the word *patient*:

main clause	*subordinate clause*
This is the patient	*who, when I visited the hospital yesterday, stopped breathing for several minutes.*

It's worth spending a little more time with subordinate clauses because no matter how long they are they have the ability to function as nouns, adjectives and adverbs. Understanding this should help you construct more precise and efficient sentences.

We recognise three kinds of subordinate clauses:

NOUN CLAUSE – where the clause acts as a noun.

*She told him **what she thought**.*

***What's right** and **what's wrong** are the questions at the heart of true civilisation.*

*I told him **that Judy was coming**.*

ADJECTIVAL CLAUSE – where the clause acts as an adjective.

*This is the door **that won't close properly**.*

*The parcel **that's just arrived** is for you.*

*London is the place **which offers the greatest opportunities**.*

ADVERBIAL CLAUSE – where the clause acts as an adverb.

*You should go there **before the shops open**.*

***Because it began to rain** I had to buy an umbrella.*

*We were quite upset **when John came in**.*

Look at the **noun clauses** closely and you will see that they really do function as nouns. Try mentally rewriting the sentence *She told him what she thought* as *She told him [thoughts]* and – *Presto!* – the clause becomes a noun.

Do the same for the **adjectival clauses**. What the sentence *This is the door that won't close properly* is saying is, *This is the [jammed]*

door. The adjectival clause *that won't close properly* is merely
substituting for the adjective *jammed*. Incidentally, you may have
noticed that the adjectival clauses are introduced by the **relative
pronouns** *that* and *which*. These and *who*, *where*, *whose*, *what* and *as*
are typically used for this purpose, which is why you may
sometimes see adjectival clauses referred to as **relative clauses**.

Functioning as adverbs, the **adverbial clauses** give us
information about time, place and purpose. The sentence *You should
go there before the shops open* could be saying *You should go there [now,
soon, quickly]* – all of which are adverbs. In this case, however, the
adverbial clause *before the shops open* may have been chosen over a
simple adverb as being more informative. This is the real point of
adverbial, adjectival and noun clauses – they enable us to add
unlimited shades of information and meaning to our sentences.

Misplaced Clauses

There is also another important point in knowing about
clauses and how to use them – and that is how not to *misuse* them.
Unfortunately clauses that are placed incorrectly in sentences are
not uncommon, and can cause great confusion, not to mention
embarrassment and hilarity. The BBC once carried a breathless
report about a Russian demonstration, where protestors

> *who lay down outside the Kremlin . . were carried away
> bodily singing hymns by the police.*

However, hymn-composing Russian policemen appear to
have more class than their British counterparts who were recently
called out to subdue a young lady, the result of which was that
'She was arrested by police wearing no knickers' (also BBC).

A similar state of undress was promised in another case of a
misplaced clause when The Times reported that 25 women were
planning to compete in the London Marathon 'wearing nothing

but a Wonderbra above the waist'. A hurried consultation with the organisers eventually sorted it out: rather less outrageously the women planned to run 'wearing nothing above the waist but a Wonderbra'.

Perhaps one of the most notorious misplaced clauses occurred in a report also in The Times, in which a young woman was fined by magistrates for falsely accusing a man of rape. The report went on to state that she 'claimed he had raped her twice to avoid getting into trouble for arriving home late.'

How this got through the serried ranks of sub-editors is anyone's guess, but it certainly provided readers with a baffling mental picture of the alleged rapist apologising to his parents for being late home and offering the excuse that he had to rape someone twice. Perhaps what was really meant was that 'to avoid getting into trouble for arriving home late, she claimed that a man had raped her twice'.

Don't let a clause be the cause of confusion!

Naming Things: Nouns

Nouns make up by far the biggest family of words in the English language. This is because nouns name things; everything, everyone, almost every place in the world has a name. The common and scientific names of all the plants and creatures in the natural world – from moss to mighty oaks, from insects to elephants, from mites to molluscs – add a few more million to the pile. There are nearly four billion people living in the world and all of them have one or more names. Not all human names are unique, of course; Korea is dominated by just four surnames, and in China combinations of surnames and given names are often shared by several hundred thousand individuals, but it still adds up to a mind-boggling total. The names or titles of every book written, every song composed, every movie made and every product marketed help to expand this colossal lexicon by tens of thousands of new names every day of our lives.

So although our everyday working vocabulary of pronouns, verbs, adjectives and so on remains more or less static year after year, new nouns continue to cascade into our memories, so that someone with a working vocabulary of several thousand non-noun words might have memory access to a hundred thousand common and proper nouns.

All names are nouns, but not all nouns are names. We have a habit of grabbing all sorts of words and turning them into nouns. They're sometimes well disguised, so beware:

> *She was always on the side of the **dispossessed**.*
> *He ordered the **destruction** of the French Fleet.*
> *Give me your **tired**, your **poor**, your huddled masses . . .*
> *You can have any colour providing it's **black**.*
> *He promised to show me the **way** to happiness.*

And just as adjectives and verbs can become nouns, so nouns can function as adjectives and verbs. In the 'Spot the Nouns' exercise at the start of this chapter, *American Airline peanuts* is a noun phrase with the proper noun *American Airline* acting as an adjective identifying the noun *peanuts*. The same applies to *bread and butter* in the phrase *bread and butter pudding*, where *bread and butter* (normally two nouns) become an adjective modifying the noun *pudding*.

Common and Proper Nouns

Perhaps the most important distinction we make among nouns is that some are **common nouns** and some are **proper nouns**:

COMMON NOUN	PROPER NOUN
car	Jaguar
aircraft	Boeing 747
vacuum cleaner	Hoover
country	Britain
mushroom	garicus campestris
singer	Madonna

It's a basic distinction that separates the general from the particular. **Common nouns** describe groups or members of groups while **proper nouns** identify a unique example. There are many *countries*, but only one *Britain*. There are many makes of *aircraft*, but only one called the *Boeing 747*.

Proper nouns are invariably capitalised and common nouns are not, but there are exceptions. Curiously, we capitalise words like *Saturday* and *September*, but not the seasons: *summer*, *autumn*, *winter* and *spring*.

Having established that other word classes can disguise themselves as nouns, and that nouns can often change themselves into adjectives and verbs, how can we tell when a word is really a noun? One way is to place a determiner in front of the word, such as *the*, *a* or *an*:

NOUNS	NON-NOUNS
a **racehorse**	a **racing**
the **park**	the **parked**
an **assembly**	an **assemble**
some **cash**	some **cashable**

Other tests include a noun's ability to take on singular and plural form (try to pluralise the non-nouns above: you can't); to be replaced by pronouns (*he*, *she*, *it* etc); and to accept add-ons to form new nouns:

book / booking / booklet / bookman / bookmark / bookshop

More strikingly, nouns have the ability to 'possess', to indicate ownership:

*My **assistant's** desk*
*The **president's** concern*
*His **uncle's** death*
*It's **yesterday's** news*

Nouns can also be **concrete nouns**, the names of things we can see and touch, or **abstract nouns**, which describe concepts, ideas and qualities:

CONCRETE NOUNS   *earth, sky, vapour, girl, window, concrete*

ABSTRACT NOUNS   *instinct, strength, coincidence, existence, Christianity*

Both common and proper nouns have **gender**, too, which we learn to distinguish from a very early age:

	MASCULINE	FEMININE	NEUTER
Common nouns	*boy, bull, cock, stallion, grandpa*	*woman, cow, hen, mare, actress*	*letter, box, gun, house, sky*
Proper nouns	*Frank Sinatra, Peeping Tom*	*Joan of Arc, Cleopatra*	*Xerox, Aida, China, Ford*

There are a few nouns that defy this three-way gender classification for which we might invent a fourth type: **dual**

gender: *parent, cousin, teacher, student, horse,* etc.

Another class of noun familiar to everyone is the **compound noun** – again demonstrating a noun's potential to grow:

> *gin and tonic, scotch on the rocks, grass-roots, Eggs McMuffin, mother-in-law, attorney general, Coca-Cola, swindle sheet.*

Still another fascinating quality of the noun is its capacity to be countable or uncountable.

Countable and Uncountable Nouns

A **countable noun** is usually preceded by a determiner such as *a, an* or *the*, and can be counted. It can also assume singular or plural form:

*a **hamburger***	*five **hamburgers***	*several **hamburgers***
*an **egg***	*a dozen **eggs***	*a nest of **eggs***
*the **mountain***	*the two **mountains***	*the range of **mountains***
*a **salesperson***	*three **salespersons***	*a group of **salespersons***

Uncountable nouns, as the name suggests, cannot be counted; nor do they have a plural form:

> *music, poetry, cement, light, luck, greed, geography*

But be careful here, because nouns, including uncountable nouns, are slippery. Take the uncountable noun *light*, as in the sentences *There was **light** at the end of the tunnel*, or, *Eventually he saw the **light***. But in a different context, *light* becomes a countable noun: *The ship was lit by many bright **lights***.

Other seemingly uncountable nouns can be counted, too. Take *bread*. It is not unusual to read these days that some bakeries carry 'up to 50 varieties of breads'.

We can also quantify non-count nouns such as *bread*; we can have *slices, pieces, bits, chunks, lumps, ounces* and even *crumbs* of bread. Or take *music*. We can get around its uncountability to some extent by using such terms as *a piece/fragment/snippet/*etc. *of music*.

Singular and Plural Nouns

Of all the chameleon qualities of the countable noun, its capacity to exist in singular and plural forms is perhaps the most interesting and certainly – for most of us – the most perplexing.

Singulars and plurals have for a century or two provided wordsmiths and gamesters with a playground for puzzles like these:

- Name words ending in *-s* which are spelt the same in singular and plural forms. (Answer: *shambles, congeries*)

- Name the plural of a noun in which none of the letters are common with the singular. (Answer: *cow = kine*)

- Name any plural words with no singular. (Answer: *scissors, jeans, trousers, knickers, binoculars, spectacles, marginalia,* etc.)

In the last category you could include the uncountable nouns known as 'mass nouns' (*police, poultry, timber, grass, cattle, vermin, manners, clothes,* etc.) which are, in a sense, plurals without singulars. If it's beginning to dawn on you that the singular/plural double act is littered with inconsistencies, you would be right.

But there *is* a sort of system. Most nouns change from singular to plural by the simple addition of an *-s*:

shop, shops   *boat, boats*   *girl, girls*   *cloud, clouds*

This is by far the largest group. Notice, by the way, that

there are no apostrophes before the -*s*. Then there is another, smaller group that requires an added -*es* to become a plural:

circus, circuses   *bush, bushes*   *tomato, tomatoes*   *bus, buses*

So far, so good. But now we come to other – fortunately smaller – groups that pluralise in quaint and random ways:

mouse, mice	*loaf, loaves*	*tooth, teeth*	*foot, feet*
child, children	*ox, oxen*	*lady, ladies*	*wife, wives*
oasis, oases	*man, men*	*wharf, wharves*	*index, indices*

Foreign-derived words – mostly Greek, Latin and French – have their own rules concerning plurals:

phenomenon, phenomena	*medium, media*	*tempo, tempi*
alumnus, alumni	*formula, formulae*	*bureau, bureaux*
automaton, automata	*datum, data*	*criterion, criteria*
paparazzo, paparazzi	*kibbutz, kibbutzim*	*graffito, graffiti*

One small group that plays tricks consists of words that are plural in form but singular in meaning: *news, economics, acoustics, premises, thanks, savings.* What's confusing about these is that some take a singular verb (*the news that night **was** bad; acoustics **is** a much misunderstood science*) while others require a plural verb (*the premises **were** empty; her entire savings **have been** stolen*).

Another bunch that lays trip-wires are the compound nouns:

Is it *two gins and tonic, please, two gin and tonics,*
or *two gins and tonics?*

Is it *poet laureates* or *poets laureate?*

Is it *mother-in-laws* or *mothers-in-law?*

Is it *scotches on the rocks,* or *scotch on the rocks's?*

Is it *Egg McMuffins* or *Eggs McMuffin?*

These are conundrums that have tortured us for ages. There is, however, a view, which sounds reasonable, that hyphenated compounds should be pluralised by adding an *-s* at the end (*forget-me-nots, stick-in-the-muds, 15-year-olds*) with, strangely, the exception of *mothers-in-law*; and that unhyphenated compounds should have the *-s* added to the central or most important noun. If we follow this advice, we get *gins and tonic, poets laureate, scotches on the rocks* and *Egg McMuffins* (it is the McMuffin bit that creates the difference, not the eggs).

But inconsistencies will still pursue us. Some people (including newspaper and book publishers) will hyphenate compounds such as *gin-and-tonic* and some won't. You will also see *right-of-way, right of way, rights-of-way, right-of-ways* and even *rights-of-ways* – so who's right? Similar arguments surround *spoon full* and *mouth full*, and *spoonful* and *mouthful*. The plurals of the first pair are straight-forwardly *spoons full* and *mouths full*. But the meanings of the second pair are different; here the attention is on the fullness of a single spoon or mouth, so *-ful* is the central or important part of the compound and should have the *-s* added to it: *spoonfuls* and *mouthfuls*. But remember that these recommendations are not bound by strict rules; many grammarians will opt for *spoonsful* and *mouthsful* and *mother-in-laws*, and will expect to be served like anyone else when they ask the barman for two *gin-and-tonics*.

Collective Nouns

Collective nouns identify groups of things, people, animals and ideas:

audience, council, staff, team, enemy, collection, herd, quantity

The effect of a collective noun is to create a singular entity which, although many creatures (bees in a *swarm*), people (members of a *jury*) or objects (a *number* of entries) are involved, should be treated as a singular noun:

> *The **army is** outside the city gates.*
>
> *Will **this class** please behave **itself**?*
>
> *The **management has** refused to meet us.*

Sometimes, however, a collective noun is a bit equivocal, taking singular or plural form according to context. Unsurprisingly, this can lead to confusion:

> *A vast **number** of crimes **is/are** never reported at all.*
>
> *The **majority is/are** in favour of the merger.*

Such collective nouns sometimes lead to grammatically correct but odd-sounding emissions such as ***none** of us **is** going to work today*, and *a **lot** of things **is** wrong with the world*, and this has led to the relaxation of the old rule of always following a collective noun with a singular verb. This makes sense when the context refers to individuals within the group, rather than the group as a whole. Look at this sentence in which *family* is the collective noun:

> *The **family was** given just one week to find a new home.*

Here the family is treated as a single entity and the noun is therefore followed by a singular verb – *was*. But there are occasions when a family can be viewed more as a number of individual members:

> *The **family were** informed that if **their** aggressive behaviour continued, **they** would be evicted.*

In this case the writer assumes two things – first, that the family did not act aggressively as a unit, as an army would, but that aggressive acts were carried out by members of the family, and not necessarily all of them; and, second, that the members of the

72

family were not necessarily consulted or warned *en masse*, but individually – not an unreasonable assumption. In this context, therefore, *family* has a very strong case for requiring a plural verb and pronouns.

Too often, however, collective nouns are followed by plural verbs willy-nilly, regardless of context. *The Times* recently carried this front-page report: 'Diplomats like to stress the BBC *are* seen in Riyadh as the voice of the British establishment . . .' And again: 'Michael Howard, the Home Secretary, said: "The Daily Mail *haven't* done anything against the law . . . " ' In these contexts it is very difficult to see how the BBC and the *Daily Mail* can be anything but singular entities.

Many caring users of English are beginning to complain about this creeping plurality of collective nouns. Here are some more examples, all from national newspapers:

> *A team were forming, the captain was in command, a spinning pitch had been prepared . . . (The Sunday Times)*

> *Your committee of ten are about to take a trip . . . (Daily Telegraph)*

> *. . . the family who own the site charge admission . . . (Daily Telegraph)*

> *. . . the leadership have decided . . . (Daily Telegraph)*

> *The Government are absolutely clear that the right . . . (The Times)*

And this quite baffling sentence: 'Railway are dying' (*The Times*). Of course individual writers and publications will continue to differ on how to treat collective nouns, but this liberalisation inevitably leads to sentence discord and confusion. An example of this was given in the chapter on *Sentences* (page 44) but here is another.

In an article on the 'Americanisation of Europe' *The Observer* could not make up its mind whether McDonald's was corporately collective or not:

> *. . . McDonald's **are** well used to the accusation . . . the trouble with McDonald's is that everybody has an opinion about **it** . . . yet McDonald's, with **its** training 'universities' . . McDonald's **has** become a symbol . . . yet McDonald's stress that **they** go out of their way . . .*

A real mess, isn't it?

Regardless of your views on the merits or otherwise of the 'institutional plural' it is important that, once you are committed to a singular or plural verb, you don't change in midstream:

NOT	*The Tilner Committee **has** a week in which to announce **their** findings.*
BUT	*The Tilner Committee **has** a week in which to announce **its** findings.*
OR	*The Tilner Committee **have** a week in which to announce **their** findings.*

It's also worth mentioning a quite minor category of nouns that can cause bewilderment – noun clauses in which two nouns, including plural nouns, combine to form a single entity, and which usually take singular verbs:

> *Bacon and eggs **is** always served at the Sportsman's Cafe.*
> *Tripe and onions **seems** to be disappearing from British menus.*
> *Two months **is** too long for the school holidays.*
> *Whisky and soda **was** his favourite tipple.*

Collective nouns aren't always so mind-bending. Knowing the correct collective labels for groups of birds, animals and humans can score you points at quiz nights. There are hundreds of them; here are a few:

A **murder** *of crows*	A **convocation** *of eagles*
An **exaltation** *of larks*	A **chattering** *of starlings*
A **dray** *of squirrels*	A **knot** *of toads*
A **business** *of ferrets*	A **charm** *of finches*
A **gaggle** *of geese (on water)*	A **skein** *of geese (when flying)*
A **colony** *of penguins*	An **ostentation** *of peacocks*
A **clamour** *of rooks*	A **parliament** *of owls*

Those are traditional English terms of long standing. But the urge to collectivise has led to some more recent, whimsical creations:

A **rash** *of dermatologists*	A **piddle** *of puppies*
A **descent** *of in-laws*	An **overcharge** *of plumbers*
A **fraid** *of ghosts*	A **failing** *of students*
An **innuendo** *of gossips*	A **slew** *of dragons*

How Nouns Become Possessive

We have seen that when we pluralise most nouns, we add an *-s* (*ghost*, *ghosts*). Note, no apostrophe. But when a noun changes to its possessive form, we indicate this by adding an *-'s*. Note the apostrophe:

a ghost	*a ghost's shroud*
the team	*the team's triumph*

Where common singular nouns end with *-s* (*bus*, *atlas*, *iris*) we add an apostrophe after the *-s*:

the bus's route	*the atlas's value*	*the iris's colour*

For common plural nouns ending with *-s* (*girls*, *paintings*) or nouns plural in form but singular in meaning (*ashes*, *bagpipes*,

75

works) we simply add an apostrophe – in effect an apostrophe inserted between the end of the word and an invisible second -*s*:

> *The invitation went out for the **girls'** party.*
> *The **paintings'** ownership was being contested in court.*
> *She objected to the **bagpipes'** capacity to disturb her sleep.*

With proper nouns ending in -*s* (*Jesus, James, Jones*) we have the option of adding the -*'s*, or simply adding an apostrophe after the final -*s* of the name:

> *They decided to go to **James's** party after all.* (or *James'*)
> *The **Jones's** house was always kept spick and span.* (or *Jones'*)

As many of us find that apostrophe spells catastrophe there is a more detailed session on the contentious 'upstairs comma' in *Punctuation*: *Symbols of Meaning* on page 188.

You, Me and other Pronouns

As we saw in the chapter on *The Building Blocks of Sentences*,
pronouns are versatile stand-ins or substitutes for nouns and noun
phrases. We also noted how they spread like a rash through our
speech (there are a dozen in the four short sentences in the *Pick the
Pronouns* test above) yet at the same time can cause us no end of
problems. But before we worry ourselves too much about problem-
atical pronouns, let's find out what they are.

Pronouns work like this:

Jerry went to the pub, where *he* got quite tipsy.
   | |
antecedent   pronoun

pronoun for Julie
|

Julie saw the *tulips* *she* wanted, as *they* were the deep purple *she* loved.
 | | | |
antecedent antecedent   pronoun for tulips   pronoun for Julie

That demonstrates the basic way in which pronouns function,

even when there appears to be no antecedent in a sentence:

***Who** would have imagined **it** would come to **this**?*

Help! Where are the antecedents for *Who*, *it* and *this*? What is happening is that the three pronouns are standing in for three 'ghost' antecedents. Let's try to construct a sentence that might have preceded the above sentence, with all antecedents present:

The coach, the team and all the supporters would never have imagined that kicking an umpire would result in the captain being banned for a year.

That sentence spells out all the facts without any pronouns. Now identify the antecedents and their matching pronouns:

The coach, the team and all the supporters – antecedent for the pronoun *Who*.

kicking an umpire – antecedent for the pronoun *it*.

the captain being banned for a year – antecedent for the pronoun *this*.

You should now clearly see that if the first sentence had been preceded by a sentence similar to the information-packed second sentence, it would have made perfect sense with just its three pronouns.

We recognise and constantly use eight types of pronouns:

- **PERSONAL PRONOUNS** – *I, me, you, she*

- **POSSESSIVE PRONOUNS** – *her, their, ours*

- **REFLEXIVE PRONOUNS** – *myself, yourselves*

- **DEMONSTRATIVE PRONOUNS** – *these, that*

- **INTERROGATIVE PRONOUNS** – *who?, which?*

- **RELATIVE PRONOUNS** – *that, whose, what*

- **INDEFINITE PRONOUNS** – *all, any, someone*

- **RECIPROCAL PRONOUNS** – *one another, each other*

A RASH OF PRONOUNS

PERSONAL PRONOUNS

We use these to identify ourselves and others and they are probably the most commonly used of all pronouns. Nevertheless it is important to know *how* to use them. Fortunately we learn what personal pronouns are for in early childhood, but imagine how someone with only a basic knowledge of English might use them:

> *I look at she,*
> *Her look at me;*
> *Her see much not,*
> *Me see quite lot.*

Personal pronouns are used in three ways:

- In the **first person,** the most intimate, which includes the person or persons doing the speaking or writing: *I, me, we, us.*

- In the **second person,** which embraces those who are being addressed or spoken to: *you.*

- In the **third person,** or 'all the others'– those who are being spoken about: *he, him, she, her, it, they, them.*

With the exception of *it*, which refers to things (although sometimes to babies and animals), all personal pronouns refer to people, while *them* can refer to people or things. There are some exceptions: a ship is customarily not an *it*, but a *she* or a *her*.

Problems with Personal Pronouns

Using personal pronouns is usually a straightforward business – except when used in certain combinations, when all hell breaks loose. Despite reams having been written about *you and me, you and I, he/she and me, he/she and I, us and we,* a good many of us remain determinedly confused.

PROBLEMS WITH PERSONAL PRONOUNS

To understand and avoid problems with these pronouns it may help to refer back to the chapter on *Let's Look at Sentences.* There we recognised that a sentence has two major components: a subject and a predicate (page 30) or, looked at in another way, a subject and an object or objects. Both subjects and objects, whether direct or indirect, can include pronouns, and here it helps to know that some pronouns are used in subject positions in a sentence, and some in object positions:

PRONOUNS SERVING AS SUBJECTS: *I, you, he, she, it, we, they, who, whoever*

PRONOUNS SERVING AS OBJECTS: *me, you, him, her, it, us, them, whom, whomever*

It is when the subjective form of a pronoun is used in an objective position that trouble starts. Take the phrase *between you and I*. Shakespeare famously used it ('All debts are settled between you and I' – *The Merchant of Venice*) and today it is commonly accepted. Grammatically, however, it is incorrect. *Just between you and I, Lucy has a secret* is wrong because *Lucy* is the subject and the preposition *between* should be followed by the objective forms of the pronouns, *you* and *me*.

But *you and I* can be grammatically correct when used in a different construction. *You and I are having the day off*, for example, is correct because *you and I* are the subjects of the sentence.

Here's another sentence which your ear will tell you is wrong:

Ask Tony and I for any further information you need.

To correct this you need to recognise that *Ask* is the subject and the phrase *Tony and I* is the direct object, because *Tony and I* are receiving the action as the result of the verb *ask*. As *I* can only be used in a subjective position it is therefore wrong, and should be the objective pronoun *me*: *Ask Tony and **me** for any further information you need*. There's a simple 'ear' test for such sentences – omit mention of any other names and you get *Ask I for any further information you need*, which is patently wrong.

Another quick test is to think of *you and I as **we***, and *you and me* as ***us***:

WRONG   *You and me are going to be late. (**us** are going to be late)*

RIGHT   *You and I are going to be late. (**we** are going to be late)*

WRONG   *They're calling you and I liars. (they're calling **we** liars)*

RIGHT   *They're calling you and me liars. (they're calling **us** liars)*

In other words you can mix and match pronouns that serve as subjects (*we and they, she and I, he and she, he and I,* etc.) and those that serve as objects (*me and him, me and her, us and them,* etc.) but not subject pronouns with object pronouns (*she and him, we and them, he and her, they and us,* etc.).

A similar test can be applied to the troublesome duo *we* and *us*:

Us vintage car enthusiasts are going to be hit hard by the new tax.
[Drop *vintage car enthusiasts* and you get *Us are going . . . !*]

It's no good telling we poor farmers about export prices.
[Drop *poor farmers* and you get *It's no good telling we about . . .*]

The Generic Personal Pronoun 'One'

The indefinite pronoun *one* is used as a personal pronoun in two ways:

● As a pronoun standing for an average or generic person, as in *One can be the victim of aggressive neighbours without any reason.*

● As a pronoun substituting for the personal pronoun *I*, as in *One is always being invited to openings but one simply can't attend them all.*

Most speakers and writers in English tend to regard either use as affected. Still, there is no valid reason for discouraging its use as in certain circumstances it can render a certain elegance to expression.

If you do use *one*, however, make sure you maintain sentence harmony by following through with *one's* (for *my, our*), *oneself* (*myself*) and *oneselves* (*ourselves*) and not mixing in clashing pronouns such as *my, you, our,* etc.

The Versatile Personal Pronoun 'It'

In our list of pronouns that serve as subjects and objects you may have noted that, like *you*, the pronoun *it* can perform both as a subject pronoun and as an object pronoun. And for a personal pronoun *it* seems to be used in 1001 different impersonal ways! *It* is truly a multipurpose pronoun.

We use *it* to refer to all or parts of a sentence, where *it* anticipates the antecedent (**It** *is a pity she is not going to sing tonight*); to refer to a previous statement, which becomes the antecedent (*Are you coming tonight? I'm thinking about* **it**); to fill in a space with no particular meaning (*Jenny hated* **it** *here; It is pointless to travel further; I think* **it** *is going to rain*). We also habitually use it in a ghostly form – by dropping it altogether:

Looks like rain.	*(It) Looks like rain.*
Do you like it? Yes, tastes good.	*Yes, (it) tastes good.*

POSSESSIVE PRONOUNS

These indicate possession or ownership and are sometimes called **possessive adjectives**. Some are used as determiners, and are dependent on nouns:

> *my groceries, her hairdresser, his anger, our house, your car, their washing machine*

while other possessive pronouns are used on their own:

> *it is ours, it is mine, theirs is out of date, his is that one, hers is over there*

Notice that possessive pronouns do not need apostrophes to indicate possession. Do not fall for the unfortunately too common errors: *it's **our's**, have you seen **their's**,* etc.

REFLEXIVE PRONOUNS

This tribe, so called because they 'reflect' the action back to the self, or subject, insinuates its members into our lives in various ways:

> *Look after **yourself**, they keep to **themselves**, **myself** included.*

Other reflexive pronouns are *herself, himself, itself, yourselves, ourselves*. And if you have a good biblical ear, you'll recognise the archaic *thou, thee, thy, thine* and *ye* as reflexive pronouns.

Some grammarians recognise a sub-group called **intensifying pronouns** which are used to emphasise, or sometimes clarify, a meaning:

> *The programme, consisting of tunes **he himself** selected, was too long.*
> *Although the aircraft was declared faulty, the **engine itself** never missed a beat.*
> *The **various committees** wouldn't **themselves** promise a more democratic style of government.*

DEMONSTRATIVE PRONOUNS

These help us to demonstrate something, or to point out things:

> *I'll take **this**.   Look at **that**!   **These** will do.   **Those** are stale.*

You'll note that these statements make sense only when the reader (or listener) has been made aware of the pronouns' antecedents. For example, if those sentences were uttered in a bakery, with the speaker pointing to various items, there would be little doubt about the meaning of the statements:

> SPEAKER (choosing a loaf): *I'll take* **this**. (pointing to a large iced birthday cake): *Look at* **that***!* (picking up some buns): **These** *will do.* (Gesturing to some tarts as she leaves the shop): **Those** *are stale.*

In writing, however, the reader should not be left in doubt as to the identity of what it is the pronoun is supposed to be possessive about.

INTERROGATIVE PRONOUNS

We use these to ask questions: *who, what, which, whose, whom*:

Who *is she, anyway?*   **Which** *one?*   **Whose** *are these?*   **What** *is it?*

You'll notice that all these are direct questions, which require question marks. However we can also use interrogative pronouns to introduce indirect questions which are *not* followed by question marks:

> *The reporter wanted to know* **who** *saw the accident.*
> *He wondered* **what** *they were going to do with the body.*

You will often see *what* used in a way that's hardly interrogative: **What** *a load of nonsense! Oh,* **what** *a lovely war.* **What** *beautiful eyes you have.* In these examples, *what* jumps out of the pronoun class and becomes an **exclamative determiner**.

Who or Whom: That is the Question!

Who is a subject pronoun; *whom* is an object pronoun – and if you make them stay in their proper places you'll have no trouble with this troublesome pair. They must also match similar subject and object pronouns: **who**/*he/she/we/they* and **whom**/*him/her/us/them*. Your ear should immediately tell you if you have applied this logical rule correctly or not:

WRONG   **Who** shall it be? (Should it be **he**? Should it be she?)

CORRECT   **Whom** shall it be? (Should it be **him**? Should it be **her**?)

WRONG   **Whom** do you think is cheating? (*Do you think **him** is cheating?*
Do you think **her** is cheating? (*Do you think **them** are cheating?*)

CORRECT   **Who** do you think is cheating? (*Do you think **he** is cheating?*
Do you think **she** is cheating? (*Do you think **they** are cheating?*)

In practice, however, *who* invariably doubles for *whom* and few people seem to mind or even notice. There are some constructions, though, where substitution is difficult (*From **whom** did you catch your cold? She was pleased with her pupils, **whom** she thought had tried really hard*) and where reconstruction can be clumsy: **Who** *did you catch your cold from? She was pleased with her pupils **who** had tried really hard, she thought.*

The rules for *who* and *whom* also apply to *whoever* and *whomever*.

RELATIVE PRONOUNS

These are *that, which, who, whom, whose, whatever, whoever* and *whomever*, and we use them to introduce relative clauses, as in *It was Clarissa **who** told me first*. We use relative pronouns indiscriminately and, with some exceptions, with confidence:

> *The suit **that** he was supposed to mend is ruined.*
> *I wish I knew **whose** parcels were delivered by mistake.*
> *I'd like those shoes **which** I saw yesterday.*
> *She's the lady to **whom** I gave the keys.*

Can you see any traps hidden here? Taking the last example, most of us would try to avoid the formal-sounding *whom* and say something like, *She's the lady I gave the keys to*. And we're increasingly dropping *that* and *which* from sentences, so that the first and third examples would customarily be spoken as:

> *The suit he was supposed to mend is ruined.*
> *I'd like those shoes I saw yesterday.*

The relative clauses in the examples above are adjectival in use: they qualify the nouns *suit*, *parcels*, *shoes* and *lady*. But relative pronouns can also work without antecedents when they introduce relative clauses that act as nouns:

> *She thinks she can do **whatever** she likes.*
> *I think I know **whose** mistake it was.*
> *They couldn't care less about **what** I think.*

INDEFINITE PRONOUNS

This is a very large and mixed bunch of words that can be called upon to function as pronouns, taking the place of undefined persons or objects. They also have a common bond, which you should spot fairly quickly:

all, any, every, everything, each, some, one, both, either, neither, few, little, less, least, many, everyone, someone, no one, something, anybody, nobody, more, most, nothing, enough, plenty, several.

The bond? They all have to do with number or quantity: nothing at all, a little, some, enough, or plenty. Here are a few pointers on using them:

- Note that pronouns such as *little*, *less*, *some*, *none* and *more* indicate portions and should only be applied to uncountable nouns (*a **little** sugar*, but not *a **little** cakes*; ***much** trouble*, but not ***much** problems*; ***less** fat* but not ***less** calories*).

- Always decide whether your antecedent is singular or plural, and then choose a pronoun to agree with it. Note that *each*, *one*, *either*, *neither*, *someone*, *anyone*, *no one*, *nobody* and *something* are all singular.

- If an indefinite pronoun is used with a verb or a personal pronoun in a sentence, make sure it agrees in number: ***Each** one of us **has** problems; **Neither** of the actors could remember **his/her** lines; **Few** of the players **are** likely to turn up today.*

- Note that *no one* is the only two-word indefinite pronoun.

RECIPROCAL PRONOUNS

This is the smallest group of pronouns – just two, in fact: *each other* and *one another*. They are called reciprocal because they express a mutual, give-and-take relationship. *Each other* refers to two people or things; *one another* is usually meant to refer to more than two:

*The two children were constantly talking to **each other**.*

*The women of the district earned extra cash by taking in **one another's** washing.*

When using the possessive form of these pronouns remember that the apostrophe comes before the *-s*, not after: *each other's, one another's*.

NUMBER PRONOUNS

Although not strictly a class – numbers are perhaps more properly defined as determiners – numerals often function as pronouns. They exist in three forms: **cardinal numbers** *(5, five, 99, ninety-nine, two hundred, zero, dozen, million)*; **ordinal numbers** *(first, tenth, twenty-fifth)* and **fractions** *(half, halves, a quarter, two-fifths)*. Here are some in use as pronouns and, for comparison, as determiners:

CARDINAL PRONOUN   *I get up at **seven** every morning.*

CARDINAL DETERMINER *The kitchen was **seven** yards in length.*

ORDINAL PRONOUN   *He was one of the **first** to visit there.*

ORDINAL DETERMINER   *It was the **first** occasion I'd met the PM.*

FRACTION PRONOUN   *In our class, **half** haven't got a clue about spelling.*

FRACTION DETERMINER *Half the class simply can't spell.*

Avoid Perplexing Pronouns

A common piece of advice is to avoid using a pronoun without first introducing its antecedent, although in practice it's done all the time:

It's very difficult, **this job**. Here *it* comes! *(the bus)*

Try also to avoid using a pronoun when it results in confusion and ambiguity. It is difficult to resist trotting out the old chestnut, *She wore a flower in her hair which was yellow speckled with mauve*. The pronoun *which* probably referred to the flower, but hair comes in some amazing colours these days, so that possibility can't be ruled out. A rewrite is called for: *In her hair she wore a flower which was yellow speckled with mauve*. Here are a few more 'pronoun howlers'; try rewriting them so that the intended meaning is instantly clear:

> *Young William told his granddad he was too old to play with Lego.*
> *When Alan patted the guard dog, his tail wagged.*
> *Joyce's mother was remarried when she was sixteen.*
> *My father told his brother that he'd had too much to drink.*
> *The vet said that the rabbit's foot was healed, and we could take it home.*
> *If your baby has trouble digesting cow's milk, boil it.*
> *He loved browsing through his doctor father's old medical books so much that he eventually decided to become one.*

That and Which

The relative pronouns *that* and *which* are becoming more interchangeable despite longstanding rules about their usage. Careful writers will use *that* to define the meaning or intention of the preceding phrase or clause: *The hotel **that** Helen stayed at has burnt down*. *That* defines or identifies the hotel for us. Use *which* when the identifying information is already supplied in the sentence: *The Imperial Hotel in Brighton, **which** Helen stayed at last year, has burnt down*. Here, *which* introduces a relative clause which merely adds extra, possibly non-essential information, and which is cordoned off by commas. If you have developed a grammatical 'ear' you will readily detect the essential difference between the two.

That and Who

Whether to use *who* or *that* for persons can sometimes present a problem but, generally, *that* is used to refer to <u>any</u> persons, and *who* to a particular person: *The mechanics **that** fixed my car ought to be shot*; but – *My mate Jim, **who** was supposed to fix my car, ought to be shot*. However, using *that* for persons can sometimes look and sound odd: *To all **that** protest that this is quick-fix politics* . . . Most writers would in this instance use *who*.

Drop 'that' With Care

The common practice of omitting *that* from many sentence constructions is considered acceptable if the meaning remains clear:

> *Are you pleased [that] I bought it? I know [that] Claire will be here tomorrow.*
> *Don't you think [that] it's a beautiful car?*

All these statements are unambiguous with *that* omitted. But proceed carefully. *Mr Benton said yesterday some shares dropped as much as 20%* could mean two things: that Mr Benton made the statement yesterday (*Mr Benton said yesterday [that] some shares dropped as much as 20%*); or that Mr Benton said some shares dropped 20% yesterday (*Mr Benton said [that] yesterday some shares dropped as much as 20%*). If you were the owner of those shares you'd be mighty interested in what Mr Benton actually meant. The appropriate insertion of *that* would make either sentence crystal clear – so when in doubt, retain *that*.

The Search for the Uni-gender Third Person Pronoun

For centuries we've used *man* and *men* generically to embrace *woman* and *women* and this practice has extended to the use of *he*, *his* and *him* to include both sexes:

> *Any runner who does not finish will have **his** application for next year's race reconsidered by the committee.*

In an age where the number of female runners is at least equal to the number of their male counterparts, the use of the masculine pronoun in contexts like this, although for so long accepted, is no longer appropriate. The problem is that the English language has no gender-neutral singular pronoun that includes both men and women, an omission that hasn't gone unnoticed by the feminist movement. Feminists argue that current usage is not only biassed against women but is also illogical. Here's an example from *The Times* in which, despite the subject being a woman (Mrs Thatcher, in fact), she is referred to by the masculine pronoun *his*:

> *The Prime Minister and the Opposition Leader each received a huge cheer from **his** own side as they entered the chamber yesterday.*

So what can we do in this age of gender equality? One suggestion is to use the *his* or *her* or *his/her* formula: *Any runner who does not finish will have **his or her** application* . . . but many writers consider this to be a clumsy solution which can be intensely irritating if repeated throughout a passage.

The most accepted course today is to either reconstruct sentences to avoid the offending pronouns, or to pluralise them: *Runners who do not finish will have **their** applications* . . . This works when the subject can be pluralised, but when it can't we're forced to use plurals like *their*, *they*, *them* and *themselves* as generic singulars:

*Judgements are made about a **person's** competence on the basis of **their** ability to spell correctly.*

Here the plural *their* agrees in person with *person's* but not in number – because *a person's competence* is singular, referring to a single person's competence. Despite continuing complaints from purists most grammarians now accept the compromise as the only practical way out of the problem. Nevertheless, some cute paradoxes will persist. Which is correct, or 'more correct'?

Everyone was blowing their trumpets.
Everyone were blowing their trumpets.
Everyone was blowing their trumpet.

The answer is that none is grammatically correct, but that the first example is considered to be acceptable. Here are some more, well-known examples of pronoun disagreement. Try to rewrite them elegantly, but grammatically correctly, while avoiding sexism. Remember that *anyone*, *everyone* and *someone* are singular subjects.

Everyone immediately returned to their cars.
Someone called but they didn't leave a message.
James saw everyone before Sue noticed them.
Anyone who feels that the slimfast regime has reduced their weight, please raise your hand.

Or could you do better than the American author J D Salinger who, in his novel *Catcher in the Rye* has his character Holden Caulfield say, 'He's one of those guys who's always patting themselves on the back'.

It's a plane! It's a bird! No! It's SUPERVERB!

The verb is usually the most important element in a sentence. It is the engine that makes the sentence go. Its business, its *raison d'être*, is to express action, or to indicate a condition or a state:

ACTION	*He is **running** away.*	*She **intended** to **live** here.*
STATE	*She **loathes** rap music.*	*Gordon **looks** quite ill.*

Action verbs express what someone or something is, was or will be doing. In other words, verbs possess **tense** to help us express **time**: Although there are 12 tenses (which we'll discuss later), here is the basic trio:

PRESENT TIME	*He **listens** to her.*	*She **is** home today.*
PAST TIME	*He's **been sacked**.*	*He **was** very ill.*
FUTURE TIME	*I **will come** if I can.*	*Jeanne **will be** here.*

Verbs are among the most versatile of all our words. You can see how clever they are in these two paragraphs. The first is a fairly matter-of-fact descriptive passage:

> *The helicopter banked and almost stalled. The engines raced and the craft tilted and a body fell out of the hatch. The machine rapidly lost height and the engines failed. Only the sound of wind could be heard. Then the machine began to revolve, out of control, throwing the pilot off and finally plunging into the sea.*

That could have been a report of a helicopter accident at sea written by an aviation safety officer with just the facts in mind. Here, though, is essentially the same passage, but brought graphically to life by selective verbs:

> *Suddenly the helicopter banked, shuddered, and seemed to stall, its arms rotating wildly, scrabbling and clawing the black sky for a grip. The engines whined and screamed, the craft lurched and a body shot out of the hatch and hurtled into the void below. The machine was now losing height,*

dropping at a breathcatching rate until the engines abruptly died, their howling replaced by the eerie whistling of the wind. Then, slowly at first, the fuselage itself began to spin around the stilled rotors, gyrating faster and faster, whirling and spinning out of control, spiralling down through the tunnel of rushing air until, a few seconds after the pilot was hurled out of the cabin, the rotors disintegrated into shards of rocketing metal and the grey coffin plummeted into the heaving black water.

You can easily see how certain verbs – *shuddered, rotating, scrabbling, clawing, whined, screamed, shot, hurtled, dropping, spin, gyrating, spiralling, hurled, disintegrated, rocketing, plummeted* – contribute to this vivid, action-packed word picture. To heighten the effect even further, some writers might move the verbs into the present tense, to give the reader a 'you are here now' sensation:

> *. . . then, slowly at first, the fuselage itself **begins** to spin . . . the rotors **disintegrate** . . . and the grey coffin **plummets** . . .*

We like using verbs so much that when we don't have one to describe an action or a condition we simply create one. Notice the verb *rocketing* in the passage above; it was once created from the noun *rocket*. In fact about 20% of English verbs were once nouns, and we're still at it. Here are a few recent coinages from our verbing activities:

> *to host, to progress, to showcase, to doorstep, to hoover, to trash, to shoehorn, to video, to rubber stamp, to input, to impact, to access, to bankroll.*

Because verbs are so useful, so versatile, it's well worth finding out what they can do, and how we can put their potential to work in our speech and writing.

Regular and Irregular Verbs

Verbs are divided into two groups: **regular**, or weak verbs, of which there are tens of thousands, and slightly fewer than 300 **irregular**, or strong verbs. Regular verbs stick to certain rules, while irregular verbs live up to their name and are real wild cards, as you will see.

REGULAR VERBS	*laugh, look, advises, play, loved*
IRREGULAR VERBS	*begin, chosen, speak, freeze, shrink*

The difference between these two groups is in their behaviour when they change shape to express tense or time: present and past time. **Regular verbs** follow a pattern; the basic form of the verb simply adds an *-s*, *-ing*, or *-ed* to express a different time or mood:

BASIC FORM	*laugh, look, play, advise, push*
PRESENT	*laughs, looks, plays, advises, pushes*
PRESENT PARTICIPLE	*laughing, looking, playing, advising, pushing*
PAST/PAST PARTICIPLE	*laughed, looked, played, advised, pushed*

Irregular verbs, however, can behave quite erratically:

BASIC FORM	*begin, choose, speak, freeze, shrink*
PRESENT	*begins, chooses, speaks, freezes, shrinks*
PRESENT PARTICIPLE	*beginning, choosing, speaking, freezing, shrinking*
PAST	*began, chose, spoke, froze, shrank*
PAST PARTICIPLE	*begun, chosen, spoken, frozen, shrunk*

Irregular verbs trouble writers because they change in such unexpected ways:

> *The verse we **write** we say is **written**,*
> *All rules **despite**, but not **despitten**,*
> *And the gas we **light** is never **litten**.*
> *The things we **drank** were doubtless **drunk**,*
> *The boy that's **spanked** is never **spunk**,*
> *The friend we **thank** is never **thunk**.*
> *Suppose we **speak**, then we have **spoken**,*
> *But if we **sneak**, we have not **snoken**,*
> *And shoes that **squeak** are never **squoken**.*
> *The dog that **bites** has surely **bitten**,*
> *But after it **fights** it has not **fitten**.*

That doggerel highlights the daffy illogicality of irregular verbs. While regular verbs have only four forms, the irregular variety can have up to five – the verb *to be* has no fewer than ten – and there is no easy way of learning them. With a little patience and practice, however, they can be memorised. Here are some irregular verbs you'll come across in everyday speech and writing:

Some Disorderly, Disobedient, Deviating Irregular Verbs

BASIC FORM	PRESENT	PAST	PRESENT PARTICIPLE	PAST PARTICIPLE
arise	*arises*	*arose*	*arising*	*arisen*
awake	*awakes*	*awoke*	*awaking*	*awoken*
bear	*bears*	*bore*	*bearing*	*borne*
bid	*bids*	*bad(e)*	*bidding*	*bidden*
bite	*bites*	*bit*	*biting*	*bitten*
blow	*blows*	*blew*	*blowing*	*blown*
bring	*brings*	*brought*	*bringing*	*brought*
choose	*chooses*	*chose*	*choosing*	*chosen*

Some Disorderly Verbs (cont.)

BASIC FORM	PRESENT	PAST	PRESENT PARTICIPLE	PAST PARTICIPLE
dive	dives	dived	diving	dived
do	does	did	doing	done
drive	drives	drove	driving	driven
fly	flies	flew	flying	flown
forgive	forgives	forgave	forgiving	forgiven
freeze	freezes	froze	freezing	frozen
go	goes	went	going	gone
hang	hangs	hung/hanged	hanging	hung/hanged
kneel	kneels	kneeled/knelt	kneeling	knelt/kneeled
lay	lays	laid	laying	laid
lie (recline)	lies	lay	lying	lain
lie (untruth)	lies	lied	lying	lied
mistake	mistakes	mistook	mistaking	mistaken
quit	quits	quit/quitted	quitting	quit/quitted
sew	sews	sewed	sewing	sewn
shear	shears	sheared	shearing	shorn/sheared
shoe	shoes	shoed/shod	shoeing	shod
slay	slays	slew	slaying	slain
speed	speeds	speeded/sped	speeding	sped/speeded
spell	spells	spelled/spelt	spelling	spelt/spelled
steal	steals	stole	stealing	stolen
stink	stinks	stank	stinking	stunk
strew	strews	strewed	strewing	strewn
stride	strides	strode	striding	stridden
strike	strikes	struck	striking	struck
strive	strives	strove	striving	striven
tear	tears	tore	tearing	torn
thrive	thrives	thrived	thriving	thrived
tread	treads	trod	treading	trodden/trod
undergo	undergoes	underwent	undergoing	undergone

BASIC FORM	PRESENT	PAST	PRESENT PARTICIPLE	PAST PARTICIPLE
undo	undoes	undid	undoing	undone
wake	wakes	waked/woke	waking	woken
wet	wets	wet/wetted	wetting	wet/wetted
wring	wrings	wrung	wringing	wrung
write	writes	wrote	writing	written

Auxiliary Verbs

These are a group of words which, added to a main verb to form a verb phrase, enables us to express an amazing range of meanings. They are 'helping' verbs, an army of waiting assistants. Apart from much else, they help us to express the relationship between the information given in a sentence and the time it was uttered or enacted – in other words, a sense of time.

At the start of this chapter we saw how verbs can change to express present, past and future time: *she listens*; *she listened*; *she will listen*. Those are the three basic tenses. But there are nine more, and these enable us to express a wide and subtle range of behavioural chronology:

The Twelve Tenses:

PRESENT   *I **go** to the city once a week.*

PAST   *I **went** to the city last week.*

FUTURE   *I **will go** to the city next week.*

As you can see, these are straightforward expressions indicating present action, past action and future intention. However sometimes we need to express continuing action in these three tenses. We achieve this by using what are called **progressive forms**:

PRESENT PROGRESSIVE *I **am going** to the city to see Simon.*

PAST PROGRESSIVE *I **was going** to the city but Simon cancelled.*

FUTURE PROGRESSIVE *I **will be going** to the city again next week.*

The next set of tenses allows us to qualify the basic past and future tenses. If for example we use the past tense to say ***I went** to the city*, we are referring to an action that took place some time before the present; perhaps I went to the city last week, yesterday, or an hour ago, but since then I have returned. The action is over. But what if we need to convey the impression that I've gone to the city but haven't returned? What we need here is a tense that indicates not only past action, but past action that continues or could continue right up to the present moment:

PRESENT PERFECT *I **have gone** to the city and will be back tonight.*

PAST PERFECT *I **had gone** to the city without my briefcase.*

FUTURE PERFECT *I **will have gone** to the city by the time you get to my flat.*

You will see that the **present perfect** tense indicates that while I have gone to the city I am still there – in other words, the action that began in the past is extended to the present moment. The **past perfect** tense indicates that a past action had taken place (my going to the city) at an earlier time than another action (discovering that I'd forgotten my briefcase). The **future perfect** tense indicates that a future action (my going to the city) is likely to take place at an earlier time than another future action (your getting to my flat).

Just as the simple present, past and future tenses require

auxiliary tenses to indicate action that is or may be continuing, so do the perfect tenses:

PRESENT PERFECT PROGRESSIVE	*I **have been going** to the city for years.*
PAST PERFECT PROGRESSIVE	*I **had been going** to the city regularly until last month.*
FUTURE PERFECT PROGRESSIVE	*If I make three more trips **I will have been going** to the city every week for the past fifteen years.*

A Verbal Warning!

You should be warned that the whole business of verbs is surrounded by revisionist controversy.

What you have read about verbs in this book is mostly based on what is today called 'old grammar' in the 'Latinate tradition'. There is nothing really wrong with this, but it doesn't quite mesh with the 'new grammar' which is based on logic rather than time-honoured rules hammered out from Latin grammar.

One problem for the student, however, is that some aspects of 'new grammar' are exceedingly complex, and also in a state of academic flux, while 'old grammar' at least has the advantage of being readily understood and followed.

One big difference between the two schools is with tense. Many linguists argue that there is no logical relationship between tense and time and that expressing time is more a matter of attitude and intention. They rightly point out many inconsistencies in our traditional thinking about tense and in particular reject the idea that there is such a thing as a *future* tense. Certainly there are no future tense endings, forcing us to resort to expressions such as *will / shall / will have been / be about to* and so on. Present and past tense can be used to convey future time (*If I **go** tomorrow; if he **went*** *next week*) and present tense can refer to past time, as, say, in a newspaper headline: *Arsenal coach resigns*.

Much the same applies to the term **past participle**, which modernists avoid, pointing out that this form is not restricted to past time but can refer to the future, as in *The novel will be written next year; The gifts will be chosen tomorrow*.

You may explore these distinctions further if you wish; otherwise, carry on as before.

The Expressive Power of Auxiliary Verbs

Although auxiliary verbs can't stand on their own, they help to extend the expressive range of other verbs to an extraordinary degree. We've seen how preceding the main verb *go* with such auxiliary verbs as *will*, *was*, *am*, *will be*, *have*, *will have*, *have been* and *will have been* helps us understand when an action is, was or will be taking place. But auxiliary verbs can do much more than that.

There are two kinds of auxiliary verbs: the three **primary auxiliaries** (*be, do, has*) which often double as main verbs; and what are known as **modal auxiliaries** (*can/could, may/might, must, shall/should, will/would*) which form **verb phrases** which enable us to express a truly amazing range of meanings: whether or not something is possible; making demands; giving permission; deducing or predicting some event, and so forth. And, by following such verb phrases by negatives (*not, never*) we can express an equal range of opposite meanings. So, to the sequential variations of the verb *go* that were illustrated in the table of tenses, we can add:

I must/must not go.　　　　*I should/should not go.*

I could/could not go.　　　　*I can/cannot go.*

I might/might not go.　　　　*I may/may not go.*

Further, there are such things as 'fringe modals', so called because they are used rarely, that we can trot out to contribute other possibilities: *I ought/ought not to go. Dare I go? I used to go. I had better/better not go. I would rather/rather not go. Need I go?* . . . and so on. Thus you can see that auxiliary verbs allow us to give each of the main verbs in the English language the power to express an additional fifty meanings at least. And with an admirable economy, too.

Will and Shall

Using *will* and *shall* frequently confuses writers. The traditional rule is: *shall* and *should* are used with the first person, singular and plural, *will* and *would* with all the other persons: *I shall, we shall, he will, she will, they will, you will, it will; I should, we should, he would, she would, they would, you would, it would:*

> *We **shall** go there first thing tomorrow.*
> *They **will** be arriving here this afternoon.*

There are, however, the usual exceptions. We often switch *shall* and *will* around for emphasis: *I will! You shall!* In legal and government circles *shall* is used willy-nilly in the belief that it carries more force and compulsion: *You shall complete all forms before applying; Claimants are warned that false statements shall be subject to severe penalties.*

Because of these inconsistencies – not to mention the tortuous grammatical logic behind the rule – the traditional distinctions are now rarely observed in ordinary speech (odd exceptions being *Shall we dance? You shall die!*) and increasingly ignored in writing (in American English *shall* is hardly ever heard or seen; *will* is standard) to the extent that there is a danger of *shall* disappearing altogether, helped on its way by the use of contractions (*I'll, she'll, he'll, they'll, it'll*) which conveniently can mean either.

May and Might

Of these two auxiliary verbs, always remember that *might* is the past tense form. *May* is correct when an outcome is still unknown. *Might* is right when an *if* is lurking in the background – when we discuss something that was likely or possible on some past occasion:

WRONG   *If it had not been for the paramedics, I **may** have died.*
(Did I or not?)

CORRECT   *If it had not been for the paramedics, I **might** have died.*
(But we know that I obviously didn't!)

WRONG   *Mr Perlman **might** leave for New York tonight.*

CORRECT   *Mr Perlman **may** leave for New York tonight.*

WRONG   *Mr Perlman **may** have left last night.*

CORRECT   *Mr Perlman **might** have left last night.*

Transitive and Intransitive Verbs

The distinction between the two is that an **intransitive verb** can stand alone (*she **speaks**; I **smile**; the clock **strikes***) while nearly all **transitive verbs** won't work unless they have some sort of relationship (*he **raised** his fist; she **laid** the book on the bed.*) You can readily see that you can't just *raise* – you have to raise *something* – a glass, a shovel, a laugh – *something*. In other words, a transitive verb transfers action from the subject to the object that follows to complete the thought; an intransitive verb doesn't require an object to complete its meaning.

The test is simple. In a sentence such as *They were told the money had vanished without trace*, the verb *had vanished* is intransitive because it can stand alone: *The money had vanished*. End of story. But if we take another sentence: *The disappearance of the money caused big problems*, the verb *caused* is transitive because it transfers the action from the subject (*disappearance of the money*), which makes no sense by itself, to the object (*big problems*). Then it all makes sense.

Some verbs can be both transitive and intransitive. A person can *breathe*, as in *That smoke was awful – at last I can **breathe**!* In that sentence, *breathe* is an intransitive verb. But here it is in a dependent, transitive role: *I wish I could **breathe** some confidence into that pupil.*

The way in which intransitive and transitive verbs work isn't merely academic. It isn't unusual for even professional writers to fall into the transitive trap. In fact it's quite usual to read sentences like this one: *The Olympic hope **tested** positive for drugs.* If this means anything it means that the athlete tested himself; what it presumably meant was *The Olympic hope **was tested** positive for drugs.* A small lapse, perhaps, but such sloppiness can lead to silliness as in a newspaper report about a fire in a shop which resulted in 'customers having to evacuate on to the pavement'.

It is worth noting that in the US the verb *write* can be used transitively, as in *You should write your Congressman* or *I have written my mother several times without a reply.*

This is a carryover from the English used by early British settlers, when it was standard usage; now it is standard in the US while British English insists on *You should **write to** your MP.*

Phrasal Verbs

We have seen how auxiliary verbs can form verb phrases. But verb phrases can also incorporate prepositions or adverbs, resulting in a single, and sometimes new, meaning. We call these **phrasal verbs**: *look up, look out, look after, look for, give up, take off, look forward to, fall out, fall down.*

Do you notice an idiomatic feel about these examples? We toss them off all the time and quickly become familiar with their often confounding meanings. If we hear someone say, 'She loves to *run down* her in-laws' we don't jump to the conclusion that she's trying to kill them with her car. The same applies to such expressions as 'Do you think Mrs McDonald will *run up* a pair of curtains for me?'

Thousands of such verb phrases have acquired precise idiomatic meanings that have little or no relationship with the words that comprise them. If a lorry driver is requested to *back up* we know what is meant because we're looking at the verb *back* followed by the preposition *up*: it means *reverse this way*. But if you were advised not to get a certain person's *back up*, or asked to *back up* a friend in an argument, you have to know or be told the different meanings because you simply can't work them out by any existing system of logic.

Although many phrasal verb constructions add nothing but paradox to the original verbs (*shout down, settle up, go back on, ring up*) and although we are somehow expected to know the difference between **checking** *the speedometer* and **checking up** *on your husband*, not even gelignite will stop us from using phrasal verbs.

Verbals and Verb Phrases

By now you should know the difference between **phrasal verbs** and **verb phrases** (which we discussed under *auxiliary verbs*, p.101). But you should also be aware of the difference between **verb phrases** and **verbal phrases**, or **verbals**.

Although derived from verbs, and often looking like verbs, **verbals** (a better name than the old *verbids*) are never used as verbs in a sentence, but as nouns, adjectives or adverbs. This probably sounds confusing – but don't give up! Understanding what verbals are and how they work in a sentence will help you avoid some of the most common mistakes in the whole of grammar.

There are three kinds of verbals: **Participles, Infinitives** and **Gerunds**, and you're probably more familiar with them than you realise.

Participles

We have seen, in the discussions of regular and irregular verbs (page 98) and the various tenses (page 101), that two important parts of a verb are the present participle and past participle, as in *go* (basic verb), *going* (present participle) and *gone* (past participle). Both participle forms are used freely as verbs:

> Hilda **was going** away.   William **had gone** to the beach.

You'll notice that both participles need auxiliary verbs to work as verbs. They can't do their work as verbs on their own (*Hilda **going** away? William **gone** to the beach?*).

But although participles can't work on their own as verbs, they *can* as verbals – functioning as adjectives:

> The company paid us at the **going** rate. (adjectivally modifies *rate*)
>
> The herb farm was a **going** concern. (adjectivally modifies *concern*)

Note that when a participle is used as an adjective it sits next to its noun: **kneeling** *figure,* **driving** *rain,* **forgiven** *sinner.* The same applies even when, as a participial phrase, it roves around a sentence:

> The book, **stolen only yesterday from the library**, was on the table. (adjectivally modifies *book*)
>
> We gazed at the book, **torn to shreds**. (adjectivally modifies *book*)

The Dangling, or Misplaced Participle

Almost the whole point of acquiring an understanding of participle usage is to learn how to avoid committing that very common grammatical gaffe – the **dangling** or **misplaced participle**. Here are a few examples:

The exhibition features works by fashion photographers executed between 1940 and 1990.

Being not quite fully grown, his trousers were too long.

After descending through the clouds, London lay beneath us.

Rolf is found murdered, spurring on his friends to hunt down the drug barons responsible.

Having said that, this book will gladden the hearts of all those who like a good weepy.

We wandered around the markets for several pleasant hours, followed by the 400-odd steps leading to the castle.

These are all examples of dangling, disconnected or missing participial phrases, participles that have lost their way or lost their noun. The result, as you can see, is ambiguity and even hilarity.

Were the photographers actually executed? Have you ever seen a pair of growing trousers? Did London really descend from the clouds? If Rolf is dead it's hard to imagine him spurring on anyone, including his friends. And it's a pretty amazing book that can speak. Finally, would you care to be followed around on your holiday by 400-odd steps?

All these sentences require rewriting, either to restore the link between noun and modifying participle, or to arrive at a reconstruction in which the meaning is clear:

The exhibition features fashion photographers' works executed between 1940 and 1990.

Because he was not quite fully grown, his trousers were too long.

After we descended through the clouds, London lay beneath us.

When Rolf is found murdered, his friends are spurred on to hunt down the drug barons responsible.

The next example exhibits an extremely common error, seen almost every day in newspapers and magazines. It is not *it* or the *book* that has spoken, but the writer. But the faulty construction can be easily corrected, either by substituting *having said that* with a phrase that doesn't require a pronoun, such as *that being said*, or by using the first person pronoun:

That being said, this is a book to gladden the hearts . . .

Having said that, I believe this is a book that will gladden . . .

A number of participles are capable of laying well disguised traps for writers – particularly *including, providing, provided, depending on, following* and *followed*. In our example the past participle *followed* is not attached to any noun or pronoun in the sentence so it attempts to link itself with the 400-odd steps. The sentence should be reconstructed either by introducing a noun –

*We spent several pleasant hours wandering around the markets, followed by **the climb** up the 400-odd steps leading to the castle.*

– or by replacing the participle with a verb to explain our relationship with the steps:

*We wandered around the markets for several pleasant hours, then **climbed** the 400-odd steps leading to the castle.*

Now you know how to pick up the pieces left by mangled and dangled participles, try your hand at correcting these sentences:

> *Abraham Lincoln wrote the Gettysburg Address while travelling to Washington on the back of an envelope.*

> *Speaking as an old friend, there has been a disturbing tendency in statements emanating from Peking . . .*
> (former US President Nixon speaking to a Chinese trade delegation).

Use participles by all means, but don't let danglers do you in.

Infinitives

An infinitive is the preposition *to* followed by a verb. Or, put another way, one of the forms of a verb preceded by *to*. Infinitives can function as nouns, adjectives or adverbs:

AS NOUNS	*To err is human, to forgive, divine.*
	He admitted that to go there made him ill.
	Merely to be watched made the bird fly away.
AS ADJECTIVES	*Her desire to confess was welcomed.* (modifies *desire*)
	It's time to go. (modifies *time*)
AS ADVERBS	*He wrote the article to attract attention to the scandal.* (tells *why* he wrote the article)
	More players are using Japanese pianos to achieve a more rounded tone. (tells *how* they are using pianos)

Infinitives can be sly creatures because they sometimes omit the *to*: *Help John [to] move that heavy wardrobe; The new legislation should help [to] resolve the problems.*

Misuse of infinitives is not uncommon and occurs in much the same way as misuse of participles: they become detached from the words they are supposed to modify:

Limpets, barnacles and winkles all have devices to survive prolonged periods of immersion.

Here the infinitive to *survive* has attached itself to *devices* instead of the intended *limpets*, *barnacles* and *winkles*. A grammatically correct construction would be:

Limpets, barnacles and winkles all have devices enabling them to survive prolonged periods of immersion.

Another common mistake is to insert an infinitive inappropriately in a sentence: *The Green Hills Building Society offers its PEP as an efficient financial instrument to pursue long term gains.* On analysis this makes no sense; it suggests that the PEP will be doing the pursuing, rather than the purchaser of the PEP. What it should be saying is . . . *an efficient financial instrument with which to pursue long term gains.* Or . . . *an efficient financial instrument intended to help you pursue long term gains.*

However, of all the abuse that the infinitive suffers it is the so-called **split infinitive** that is the most prevalent, and most contentious form.

To boldly go . . . The Split Infinitive

A century or so ago it became a solecism to split an infinitive – that is to place a word (usually an adverb) or words between the *to* and the verb which creates the infinitive: *to boldly go, to madly love, to properly understand.* The reason for this is said to stem from the fact that Latin infinitives were one word, not two (e.g. *amare*, to love) and therefore impossible to split.

Gallons of metaphorical blood have been shed over this legendary grammatical no-no, most of it on the arid sands of indifference. The position today is a little clearer, but not much. While many grammarians and writers recommend allowing splitting where appropriate, others still advise against it, not merely to conform to the old rule, but because they believe an unsplit infinitive to be more elegant in a well-written sentence, and 'unlikely to offend'.

The trouble with many unsplit infinitive constructions is that they can look and sound decidedly inelegant and formal.

> *Certain Shadow Cabinet members have secured agreement from Mr Hague that they will not have publicly to renounce their views.*

Elegant? Surely to most ears *to publicly renounce* would be more euphonic. Or place *publicly* at the end: *to renounce their views publicly*.

Unsplit infinitives can also lead to ambiguity. When Sherlock Holmes told Dr Watson about a blow he received, he took the trouble to say that he "failed to entirely avoid" it rather than that he "entirely failed to avoid" it – a rather more painful experience.

On the other hand some split infinitive constructions are unnecessarily tortuous. While *She was ashamed **to so much as mention** it to her husband* might be considered acceptable to most, *You should begin **to**, **when you can find the time**, re-read* some of the classics is screaming for a rewrite: *When you can find the time you should begin **to re-read** some of the classics.*

When you find yourself straining to keep your infinitives unsplit, or detect a tendency towards ambiguity, either split the thing or, if this is unacceptable, rewrite the sentence. *The Government is attempting dramatically to increase the number of students in higher education*. What is meant, presumably, is that the proposed increase will be dramatic, but here it looks as though it is the attempt itself that is full of drama. A split infinitive – *to dramatically increase* – in this case would convey the required meaning with precision. And – *ahem!* – with no loss of elegance, either.

To split or to not split, that is the question all writers face. The decision is yours.

Gerunds

Although the gerund is really the most straightforward of the three verbals its usage is for some reason probably the most misunderstood.

We have seen how the present and past participles of verbs are used like adjectives. Similarly, present participles of verbs (ending with *-ing*) can be used as nouns. When they function as nouns we call them **gerunds**. Let's take the verb *go* and its present participle form *going*. It looks a bit unlikely that *going* can ever make it as a noun, but it can:

> *We made good **going** on the outward journey.*

> *At the President's **going** the whole panoply of state was on display.*

> *The **going** at the racetrack is good today.*

> ***Going** isn't the fun part – it's the **arriving**.*

As with these examples a gerund can stand alone as a noun, functioning as the subject of a sentence (***Running** is her favourite sport*) or as an object (*Her favourite sport is **running***). But equally, a gerund can help form a phrase that acts as a noun:

> *She enjoys **running through the woods**.*

> *Our neighbour objects to our **holding parties all night**.*

115

So far, so good. So why do many people have problems with gerunds? The problem arises because many forget that nouns or pronouns that modify gerunds must be possessive. *Mr Phillips did not like Joe smoking in the storeroom* may look about right, but it's not. Mr Phillips does not dislike Joe, but he objects to his smoking in the storeroom. To make this clear we must treat the gerund phrase (the gerund *smoking*, modified by *in the storeroom*) as a noun. That noun (*smoking in the storeroom*) is Joe's problem; it *belongs* to Joe, and therefore we must indicate that Joe possesses it: *Mr Phillips did not like Joe's smoking in the storeroom*.

A good many writers (some of whom should know better) either don't give a damn about this possessive quality of gerunds, or simply don't understand what a gerund is.

But writers such as Jane Austen never had a problem with them; *Pride and Prejudice* is in fact an excellent object lesson in their correct use:

> *His **accompanying** them was a double advantage . . . it was not to be supposed that their absence from Netherfield would prevent Mr Bingley's **being** there . . . but at last, on Mrs Bennet's **leaving** them together . . . she caught a glimpse of a gentleman . . . and fearful of its **being** Mr Darcy, she was directly retreating . . .*

Although many might find Jane Austen's writing style quaintly mannered, few would contest its elegance, nor would they challenge her grammatical skill. She certainly knew how to use the gerund – in every case the synthesised noun phrases are treated as requiring possessives: *His, Mr Bingley's, Mrs Bennet's, its*.

There's a line from George Bernard Shaw's play *Pygmalion* that could help you remember this principle, one that's more often misquoted than not. It is <u>not</u> 'It is impossible for an Englishman to open his mouth without another Englishman despising him'. It is, with the gerund *despising* treated with respect:

*It is impossible for an Englishman to open his mouth
without another Englishman's despising him.*

There will be occasions when the proper use of gerunds will
result in awkwardness, and these often lead to their omission:
'. . . one of the book's concerns is the importance of the press
bearing witness to apartheid's horrors' (*The Times*). Here, *bearing* is
a gerund and should therefore be preceded by a possessive noun –
the press's. A careful writer would probably find this clumsy; but
rather than falling into the genitive trap would reconstruct thus:
'. . . one of the book's concerns is to emphasise how important it is
for the press to bear witness to apartheid's horrors'.

The other common error with gerunds is allow them to
become orphans, screaming. "Where's my subject?"

*The new kit costs £6.50 and allows the fanbelt to be easily
installed without getting covered in grease.*

Here the gerund *getting* and its modifier *covered in grease* is an
orphan phrase looking for a subject. In its present form the sentence
is telling us that the fanbelt will get the benefit of not being covered
by grease, not the missing motorist. To make things clear it needs
to be rewritten, either with the gerund being attached to a noun
(*without the motorist's getting covered in grease*); or, better, a pronoun
(*without you getting covered in grease*); or, better still:

*The new kit costs £6.50 and allows you to install the fanbelt
without getting covered in grease.*

A Two Minute Verbal Workout

Can you recognise a disagreeable verb when you see one?
One of the key lessons in working with verbs is that they must
agree with their subjects – in number, tense and mood. Try this

two-minute test to fine-tune your skill with working with verbs. Simply choose A or B. Answers are at the end of this chapter.

1.   **A**   *Lord Henshaw's big problem is the demands of his tenants.*
     B   *Lord Henshaw's big problem are the demands of his tenants.*

2.   **A**   *Athletics give many deprived kids a great chance in life.*
     B   *Athletics gives many deprived kids a great chance in life.*

3.   **A**   *Neither of the players deserve their goals.*
     B   *Neither of the players deserves his goal.*

4.   **A**   *There're only two finalists left.*
     B   *There's only two finalists left.*

5.   **A**   *He laid on the newly-made bed.*
     B   *He lay on the newly-made bed.*

6.   **A**   *The business may have done better if it'd had a good accountant.*
     B   *The business might have done better if it'd had a good accountant.*

7.   **A**   *The bell rang three times.*
     B   *The bell rung three times.*

8.   **A**   *If I was you I'd take the job.*
     B   *If I were you I'd take the job.*

9.   **A**   *I then remembered I forgot to order the champagne*
     B   *I then remembered I had forgotten to order the champagne.*

10. **A**   *He never knew that the shortest distance between two points is a straight line.*
     B   *He never knew that the shortest distance between two points was a straight line.*

11. **A**   *The driver says that he disliked continental roads.*
     B   *The driver says that he dislikes continental roads.*

12. **A** *Strawberries with cream was served to the visitors.*

    B *Strawberries with cream were served to the visitors.*

ANSWERS

1. **A** The subject, *Lord Henshaw's big problem*, being singular, requires the singular verb *is*.   2. **A** As *athletics* is usually regarded as a plural noun it requires the plural *give*.   3. **B** *Neither* is a singular pronoun so requires the singular *deserves his* and not the plural *deserve their*.   4. **A** The plural *two finalists* requires the plural *there're* (*there are*).   5. **B** *lie* is the basic verb describing 'to recline', so *lay*, the past tense form, is correct. The word *laid* is the past tense form of a completely different verb, *lay*, which means to 'put or set down something'.   6. **B** *it'd* or *it had* indicates that the statement is in the past tense, so *might* is right.   7. **A** *The bell rang* is correct; *rung* is the past participle form requiring an auxiliary verb: *The bell was rung three times*.   8. **B** Because *If I were you* is conjectural it takes the subjunctive mood.   9. **B** Because the action of forgetting the champagne precedes in time the action of remembering, it requires the past perfect tense, *had forgotten*. 10. **A** As *the shortest distance between two points is a straight line* is a recognised fact, it should be expressed in the present tense, even though the sense of the whole sentence is in the past.   11. **B** The tenses (*says, disliked*) in the first sentence disagree.   12. **B** If the sentence had said '*Strawberries and cream*' – which is accepted as a singular unit – then the singular *was* would be correct. With the **B** sentence, *with cream* merely modifies the plural strawberries, so the plural *were* is correct.

Score.   If you scored 12 correct, consider yourself a verbal virtuoso. Ten correct would count you as proficient, but any score of less than seven would suggest that a little more study and attention might be in order.

Describing Things: Adjectives and Adverbs

Adjectives define and modify nouns and pronouns while **adverbs** do the same for verbs, adjectives and other adverbs. They are two big families of words, interrelated and often difficult to tell apart, which is why we sometimes misuse or abuse them. Nor are they always amicable; as with the Martins and McCoys or the Montagues and Capulets, a bit of inter-family feuding goes on. It's therefore useful to learn all we can about adjectives and adverbs and how we can use them to better effect.

Here's a sentence in which the meaning depends almost entirely on adjectives and adverbs:

*You're buying the **best**,*	adjective
most	adverb
***expensive**,*	adjective
exciting	participle used adjectivally
*and **arguably***	adverb

highest *performance*	adjective / noun
saloon	noun used adjectivally
car.	noun

There are four kinds of modifier in that sentence: three adjectives, two adverbs, a participle (a verb turned into an *-ing* adjective) and two nouns (*performance, saloon*) that are used in an adjectival way.

Writing a sentence like that is a bit like juggling four balls in the air, but most of us manage to do it tolerably well without too many mishaps.

ADJECTIVES AND ADVERBS:
Inter-family feuding

In the chapter on *Parts of Speech* we found that adverbs could be identified by their *-ly* endings. That's fine for adverbs with *-ly* endings, but there are many without, and there are also some adjectives with *-ly* endings. It is these that cause confusion:

ADJECTIVES	**ADVERBS**
*He is a **slow** driver.*	*He drives **slowly**.*
*She is an **early** riser.*	*She always rises **early**.*
*That's very **loud** music.*	*John's playing **loudly**.*

Further confusion is caused by the same word doubling as adjective and adverb:

ADJECTIVE	**ADVERB**
*It was a **straight** road.*	*Anne drove **straight** home.*
*She took the **late** train.*	*Brian was always **late**.*
*He read a **daily** newspaper.*	*He reads a paper **daily**.*

Obviously we must be wary of adjectives and adverbs that don't play by the rules.

We've all seen road signs that say *GO SLOW!* and perhaps wonder, on reflection, if it ought to say *GO SLOWLY!* It may be that we have a subconscious awareness that *slow* in *SLOW LANE* is an adjective, and that *slowly*, because of its *-ly* suffix, is an adverb, and therefore the sign should warn us to *GO SLOWLY*. That would be grammatically correct but the road engineer would argue the safety benefits of brevity and few today would dispute the usage. The following adverbial examples, however, are <u>not</u> regarded as good usage:

*She put her lips to his ear and spoke **soft**.*	*(softly)*
*I'm afraid I've let him down **bad**.*	*(badly)*
*That feels **real** great!*	*(really)*

Now that we've been introduced to the two families (with the usual bewilderment following such meetings: who's who, who does what, who gets on with whom) let's subject them to some closer scrutiny.

Adjectives

Here are some adjectives in use to demonstrate how free-ranging they are:

DESCRIBING SIZE   *It was a **huge** marquee.*

DESCRIBING COLOUR   *The carpet was **burgundy**.*

DESCRIBING A QUALITY   *I loved the **plush** armchairs.*

DEFINING QUANTITY   *There were **five** windows.*

DEFINING SPECIFICITY   *Did you see her **Persian** rug?*

. . . and so on.

Adjectives can precede a noun (***huge** marquee*) or follow one (*the man, **wrinkled** with age; he requested that all the journalists **present** should leave*). They can follow a number of verbs: the *be* family – *is, are, was, were, am, being, been, look, seem, become, stay,* etc. (*the carpet is **red**, William was **angry***). They can follow pronouns (*did you find anything **useful**? Is she **unhappy**?*). They can 'top and tail' a sentence (***Welsh** choir singing is justly **famous***). A few rare adjectives can stand alone after nouns (*whisky **galore**, apples **aplenty***). Adjectives can also introduce extensive adjectival phrases (*The **highly criticised 1994 Jefferson Agricultural Economics** Report came in for another battering*) and of course they can be sprinkled liberally throughout a sentence:

> *What impressed her most of all were the **three big ancient green-tinged metallic Burmese religious** statues, the **size of tree trunks**.*

A bit over the top, perhaps, but here we have no fewer than eight adjectives (the adjectival phrase *size of tree trunks* counts as one) each adding something to the description of the statues. It's worth noting that, although no strict rules exist to tell us in which order our adjectives should be, it should follow a common-sense sequence.

For example, you sense immediately that something's wrong here:

> *What impressed her most of all were the* **Burmese religious three big green-tinged ancient metallic** *statues . . .*

An acceptable rule-of-thumb for arranging your adjectives is:

1	**QUANTITY**	*five, a hundred, three-quarters*
2	**EMOTIVE**	*lovely, ugly, rare, formidable*
3	**SIZE**	*large, tiny, immense*
4	**AGE**	*old, brand new, recent*
5	**COLOUR, TEXTURE**	*ochreous, blue, smooth, waxy*
6	**SPECIFICITY**	*Jewish, Japanese, Xeroxed*
7	**PURPOSE**	*dining* table, *wine* glass

which, followed to the letter, might result in a sentence such as this:

> *The catalogue listed* **two exquisite 23in high 18th century silver Peruzzi candle** *sticks.*

The sentence packs in a lot of information but because the adjectives follow a sort of logical sequence we can efficiently absorb the facts and probably remember them better, too.

Recognising Adjectives

What makes an adjective? Some are original descriptive words such as *good, dark, hot* and *rough*, many of which have their adjectival opposites: *bad, fair, cold* and *smooth*. But tens of thousands more began life as nouns and verbs and were changed into adjectives by having various endings tacked on to them. Most are fairly easy to recognise as adjectives:

-able	*notable, fashionable, detestable, desirable*
-al	*natural, mortal, skeletal, oriental*
-ar	*jocular, circular, spectacular, singular*
-ed	*excited, crooked, married, cracked*
-ent	*excellent, indulgent, emergent, persistent*
-esque	*picturesque, Romanesque, statuesque*
-ful	*wonderful, hopeful, forgetful, thoughtful*
-ible	*sensible, comprehensible, horrible, responsible*
-ic	*heroic, psychic, angelic, romantic*
-ical	*periodical, magical, farcical, psychological*
-ish	*liverish, childish, quirkish, British*
-ive	*reflective, massive, defensive, offensive*
-less	*endless, cloudless, hopeless, legless*
-like	*lifelike, ladylike, childlike, warlike*
-ous	*nervous, herbaceous, piteous, officious*
-some	*meddlesome, awesome, loathsome, fearsome*
-worthy	*newsworthy, praiseworthy, seaworthy*

and two adjectival endings to watch for –

| -ly | *lonely, crinkly, sickly, prickly* |
| -y | *earthy, shaky, funny, tacky, kinky* |

These two endings provide a *wildly* (adverb) *bubbly* (adjective) brew of pitfalls and booby traps. Try to separate the adjectives from the adverbs among these examples:

truly   idly   gravelly   loyally   woolly   yearly
thankfully   gentlemanly   brazenly   properly   holy

If you try placing each of the words before a noun (**truly** *car*, **idly** *book*, **gravelly** *voice*) you should easily score 100%. The adjectives are *gravelly, woolly, yearly, gentlemanly* and *holy*. The rest are adverbs. It's simple if you remember that adjectives alone qualify nouns and pronouns.

Kinds of Adjective

You must be aware by now that adjectives cover a lot of ground. Nouns are always eager to spring into adjectival roles: ***book** shop*, ***lawn** seed*, ***mineral** rights*, ***orange** drink*. Adjectives breed fast. While one group of logophiles is enthusiastically creating perfectly serviceable adjectives to describe animal qualities by adding *-like* to nouns (*cat-like, ape-like, bear-like, cattle-like, thrush-like*), another bunch doubles up with Latin-derived versions: *feline, simian, ursine, bovine* and *turdine*. Even pronouns enter the fray to serve as adjectives:

POSSESSIVE ADJECTIVES	***our** home*, ***your** responsibility*, ***his** car*
DEMONSTRATIVE ADJECTIVES	***this** movie*, ***those** strangers*, ***that** dog*
RELATIVE ADJECTIVES	*I know **what** matters most. She is the woman **whose** bag was stolen.*
INTERROGATIVE ADJECTIVES	***Whose** idea? **Which** jacket? **What** smell?*
INDEFINITE ADJECTIVES	***any** person*, ***each** tree*, ***another** problem*

The adjectival ambitions of pronouns, especially demonstrative pronouns, can cause understandable confusion. 'When is a pronoun a pronoun? When is a pronoun an adjective?' you may ask. Perhaps you should remind yourself of the role of pronouns – they stand in for other nouns:

	***This** is my diary.*	*Is **that** the car you bought?*
i.e.	*This [diary] is my diary.*	*Is that [car] the car you bought?*

But these statements can be expressed differently, by using

pronouns as adjectives to modify the nouns:

> **This** *diary is mine.*   *Did you buy* **that** *car?*

You can see here that the diary is described as *mine*, and that the car I'm asking about is described as *that* car. Clearly in these two sentences the pronouns are playing their adjectival roles.

We have already witnessed the dexterity with which verbs, via their participles, can serve as adjectives – how, for example, the basic verb *go* can, through its present participle *going*, spurn its auxiliary verb (*is, was, will be,* etc.) and turn into a verbal participle, an *-ing* adjective: *We were paid at the **going** rate.* Here are some more examples:

VERB PARTICIPLE	ADJECTIVAL PARTICIPLE
The kangaroo went **springing** *away.*	*They chased the* **springing** *kangaroo.*
He hated **waking** *up in the mornings.*	*He spent all his* **waking** *hours eating.*
The fire was **roaring** *through the woods.*	*She enjoyed the* **roaring** *fire.*

There are adjectives that can roam around a sentence with considerable freedom, and others that are locked into certain positions. The former are called **central adjectives** and the latter are **peripheral adjectives**:

CENTRAL ADJECTIVE   *This is a **new** car.*
*This car is **new**.*
***New** the car may be, but it is too expensive.*

PERIPHERAL ADJECTIVE *The man spoke **utter** nonsense.*

Here you can see that utter cannot be moved to any other position (*The man spoke nonsense that was **utter**?*); its function here as an adjective is specifically to modify the noun *nonsense* (or nouns such as *amazement, fool, limit, bliss* to create well-known clichés).

Another way to look at adjectival positioning is to consider their use as **attributive** (*dark night, rank odour*) or **predicative** (*the night is **dark**, the odour was **rank***). Adjectives that can function both attributively and predicatively are usually central adjectives that can move about. But a few adjectives can only be used in a predicative way. We can write *They were filled with **sheer** terror* but not *They were filled with terror that was **sheer***.

In an earlier example we saw *Welsh* used as an adjective and noted also that *British* could act as an adjective. You could call these **proper adjectives** because they define particular things: ***Chippendale** furniture, **Shrewsbury** cake, **Scotch** whisky*. Adjectives that describe classes of things (***leafy** tree, **white** house, **angry** bull*) are of course **common adjectives**.

The E-x-p-a-n-d-i-n-g Adjective

One of the most valuable services that adjectives provide is a range of comparisons. Imagine trying to describe the comparative sizes of several people or things without *small/smaller/smallest* and *big/bigger/biggest*. Most adjectives work like that; they can express several comparative qualities: the same, less, least, more, most. With many adjectives we simply add *-er* (*taller, weaker, angrier*) or *-est* (*tallest, weakest, angriest*), but there are some that resist this convenient treatment. Even though Lewis Carroll got away with *curiouser* and *curiouser* we don't try to imitate *prettiest* with *beautifulest* or *brightest* with *colourfulest*. Instead we attach intensifiers such as *more, most, less,* and *least*: *the **most** beautiful, the **least** colourful*. An exception is *unkind*; although we don't have *unkinder* as a word, *unkindest* survives from the 16th century in the phrase ***unkindest** cut of all*.

There are, as you can see, three comparative forms of adjectives: the basic **descriptive adjective**, the **comparative adjective** (where two entities are compared), and the **superlative adjective** (where three or more entities are compared) –

DESCRIPTIVE	COMPARATIVE	SUPERLATIVE
big	*bigger*	*biggest*
loud	*louder*	*loudest*
many	*more*	*most*
few	*fewer*	*fewest*
endearing	*more endearing*	*most endearing*

Using this fairly limited range of comparisons, supplemented by intensifiers such as *quite, incredible, somewhat* and *very*, we are able to convey mental pictures of almost anything with startling verisimilitude:

> It was a **big** celebration. It was a **very big** celebration. It was the **biggest** celebration ever. It was **bigger** that any other celebration I've seen. It was **fairly big**. It was **quite big**. It was **incredibly big**. Well, it was a **biggish** celebration . . .

Watch for **absolute adjectives**, however, such as *dead, square, circular, equal, total, unique, absolute, infinite* and *impossible*. These cannot usually be modified by adverbs; after all if you've expired you can't be *more dead* or *less dead* or *dead*er! If something is *impossible*, that's it. And *unique* means exactly that: one of a kind. So you cannot have something that's *more unique* or *uniquer* than anything else.

Tips on Using Adjectives

- **Be aware of cliché adjectives.** These are what are known as 'limpet adjectives' – they always seem to stick to certain host nouns:

absolute certainty	*actual* facts	*arid* desert
audible click	*free* gift	*general* consensus
drastic steps	*full* inquiry	*lonely* isolation
mutual cooperation	*new* creation	*long-felt* want
past history	*personal* friend	*safe* haven
unexpected surprise	*widespread* concern	*utmost* urgency

● **Practice adjectival economy – 1.** Adjectives allow us to reduce verb phrases to single words without sacrificing meaning:

BEFORE *Patricia came to the party wearing a frock **that was embroidered by hand**.*

AFTER *Patricia came to the party wearing a **hand-embroidered** frock.*

BEFORE *I apologised to Margaret for my behaviour, **which I regretted**.*

AFTER *I apologised to Margaret for my **regrettable** behaviour.*

● **Practice adjectival economy – 2.** On the other hand, avoid adjectival tailbacks. Descriptive traffic jams can be self-defeating; by the time the reader has reached the last adjective, the first is probably forgotten. If you find you've written a sentence in which half the words are adjectives, try another construction.

● **Make sure your adjectives are working.** Make sure every adjective you use adds something essential to the sentence: *Her skis sliced through the **powdery white** snow on her **downward** trajectory.* Most of us know that snow is white, and believe it is quite difficult to ski uphill, so the adjectives *white* and *downward* are superfluous and can be returned to the dictionary.

Add To Your Adjectives: 2 Minute Test

Earlier we listed a range of adjectival endings: *sensible* (-ible), *childish* (-ish), *awesome* (-some) among them. But there are a few more. How many adjectives can you think of that have any of the following endings: *-ing*, *-proof*, and *-en*?

Answers:

-ing	*degrading, abiding, boring, outstanding, pending, engaging, charming, encouraging, fetching, shocking, astonishing, blushing, rollicking, reeking, appealing.*
-proof	*waterproof, rainproof, foolproof, shockproof.*
-en	*golden, wooden, sodden, molten, ashen, earthen, forsaken, broken, brazen, drunken, shrunken, silken, sullen, waxen, misshapen, barren, rotten, graven.*

Adverbs

As with adjectives, we use adverbs to add information and extra layers of meaning to a statement. Adverbs, however, are far more versatile; while adjectives can modify nouns and pronouns, adverbs are regular Houdinis, qualifying a verb here, boosting an adjective there, appearing in disguise to support another adverb – even bossing phrases and whole sentences about!

MODIFYING A VERB	*The choir sang **sweetly**.*
MODIFYING AN ADJECTIVE	*The choir sang for **almost** three hours.*
MODIFYING ANOTHER ADVERB	*The choir sang **very** sweetly.*

Because of their chameleon-like quality, adverbs, as we've already seen, can easily be confused with adjectives, which leads to incorrect usage. At the risk of being repetitious, it's worth looking again at how adverbs and adjectives disguise themselves:

ADVERBS
*The train arrived **early**.*
*Ellen hadn't **long** left home.*

ADJECTIVES
*They caught the **early** train.*
*There was a **long** queue at the ticket office.*

You should satisfy yourself right now that you know why *early* and *long* are adverbs in the first two sentences (they modify the verbs *arrived* and *left*, telling <u>when</u> the train arrived, and <u>when</u> Ellen left home) and adjectives in the second two (they modify the nouns *train* and *queue*).

How Adverbs Work

Adverbs are used to supply additional information and meaning to otherwise bald statements. They do this by:

DEFINING MANNER	*They played **happily** together.*
DENOTING PLACE	*They can play over **there**.*
FIXING TIME	*We can all go there **afterwards**.*
CONVEYING EXTENT	*We never seem to get **enough**.*
EXPRESSING FREQUENCY	*We **hardly ever** go there.*
INDICATING VIEWPOINT	*I would never go there, **personally**.*
INDICATING ATTITUDE	***Curiously**, she has never been there.*
LINK A PREVIOUS THOUGHT	***Nevertheless**, I feel we should go.*
MODIFY A STATEMENT	*It is **possibly** the best solution.*

You'll notice that while some adverbs are stand-alone words such as *there, enough, up, now, here,* and *very,* others appear to have been created from existing words. The most common of these are created by adding *-ly* to adjectives (*usually, kindly, romantically, roughly, sincerely, cheaply, quickly,* etc.) or by using existing adjectives (*friendly, early, hard, fast*) in an adverbial way. Still other adverbs are created by the suffixes *-wise* (*clockwise, otherwise*); *-wards* (*backwards, homewards*) and *-ways* (*endways, always*).

Positioning Your Adverbs

Another aspect of an adverb's versatility is its mobility in a sentence. While adjectives are fairly restricted in their movement, most adverbs can wriggle in anywhere. The linguist David Crystal has demonstrated this all-purpose quality with devastating effect, using a seven-way sentence:

1. ***Originally***, *the book must have been bought in the shop.*
2. *The book **originally** must have been bought in the shop.*
3. *The book must **originally** have been bought in the shop.*
4. *The book must have **originally** been bought in the shop.*
5. *The book must have been **originally** bought in the shop.*
6. *The book must have been bought **originally** in the shop.*
7. *The book must have been bought in the shop, **originally**.*

Not all adverbs are so flexible, however. Many feel uncomfortable in certain positions while others, wrongly placed, can convey a different meaning altogether or, at the very least, result in ambiguity. Here's a brief guide to help you position your adverbs for the intended effect:

DEFINING MANNER　　　(adverb usually at the end of sentence)

Not advised –　　　　*He rather **erratically** walked.*
Much better –　　　　*He walked rather **erratically**.*

133

DENOTING PLACE   (adverb typically at the end of
                            sentence)

    Not advised –   *Over **there** he threw the stone.*
    Much better –   *He threw the stone over **there**.*

FIXING TIME   (adverb best towards the end of
                            sentence)

    Not advised –   *I **recently** saw that movie.*
    Much better —-   *I saw that movie **recently**.*

CONVEYING EXTENT   (adverb works best in the middle)

    Not advised –   *The jar is full, **almost**.*
    Much better –   *The jar is **almost** full.*

EXPRESSING FREQUENCY   (adverb usually not at the beginning)

    Not advised –   ***Always** he is going to the pub.*
    Much better –   *He is **always** going to the pub.*

INDICATING VIEWPOINT   (adverb best placed at front of
                            sentence)

    Not advised –   *I shouldn't comment, **strictly speaking**.*
    Much better –   ***Strictly speaking**, I shouldn't comment.*

INDICATING ATTITUDE   (adverb most effective at the
                            beginning)

    Not advised –   *They both decided to **wisely** stay away.*
    Much better –   ***Wisely**, they both decided to stay away.*

A guide like this is not a rule book, for there are many
exceptions. For example, *enough* is an adverb of extent or degree
and it is commonly placed in the middle of a sentence: *I've done
enough work for the day*. But see what happens when *enough* is placed
at the beginning and end of sentences: *Do you think we've had **enough**?
Enough has been said on the subject already.* What has happened is that

in both these sentences *enough* has turned into a pronoun! Look at the sentences again and you will see that this is so.

Tips on Using Adverbs

● **Beware of misplaced adverbs.** Always keep adverbs such as *nearly, only, even, quite, just*, etc, as near as possible to the words they're meant to modify. *She **just** went to the store to buy some jeans* appears to mean that, only a short while ago, she went to the store to buy jeans. But what the statement intended to convey was, *She went to the store **just** to buy some jeans*.

● **In particular, be careful about misplacing the adverb 'only'.** This adverb is the cause of many mistakes – and misunderstandings. *Professor Hawking only published his book after years of deep thought.* Does this mean that all Professor Hawking ever did, after years of deep thought, was to publish this book? It seems so, but it isn't true. What the sentence intended to convey was *Professor Hawking published his book **only** after years of deep thought*. When using *only* make sure it is placed next to the word or phrase it modifies – in this case *after years of deep thought* and not *published his book*.

● **Avoid the 'squinting' adverbial modifier.** Ingeniously named 'squinting modifiers' by American grammarians, these are adverbs that can ambiguously attach themselves to different parts of a sentence to give two meanings: *They keep their TV going **often** without a glance all day.* Do they often have their TV on without paying attention to it, or is it on all day during which they often pay no attention to it? *Women who sunbathe **frequently** run the risk of skin disease.* Are we talking here about women running the risk of skin disease because they sunbathe too frequently, or saying that *every* woman who sunbathes runs the risk of skin disease frequently? Make sure your adverb placement conveys *exactly* what you mean.

- **Be wary of starting sentences with adverbs.** *Interestingly*, this advice is given by *The Times* to its journalists (this sentence is an example). 'Such constructions,' advises *The Times*, 'are not forbidden, but sentences starting with adverbs are normally built on sand.'

- **All is not well and good.** Many writers misuse *good* (adjective) and *well* (adverb). When we use *well* to describe the state of someone's health we use it as an adjective (*Do you feel **well**? Judith is quite **well**. Did you hear about that **well** woman programme?*) but at all other times it is an adverb that describes *how* something is done: *That horse runs **well**. Your tie goes **well** with that shirt. The medicine is working **well**.* Don't use *good* as an adverb (*Elizabeth can cook quite **good***) but always as an adjective (*Elizabeth's cooking can taste **good***).

- **Use accumulated adverbs only for effect.** There are a number of adverbial clichés which should normally be avoided but can sometimes be used for effect and emphasis: *I've told you **over** and **over** again . . **never**, **never**, go there . . . you go **on** and **on** and **on** . . . **rightly** or **wrongly** . . . I was **madly**, **crazily**, **hopelessly**, **desperately** in love.*

- **'Hopefully' is respectable.** Many writers frown over the adverb *hopefully* when it's used to mean 'let's hope' or 'it is hoped', as in *Hopefully, the team will play better next time*. Purists insist that its traditional meaning is 'full of hope'. However the respectability of the 'new' meaning can be readily defended. It originated from the German *hoffentlich*, meaning 'I hope so', which travelled with German migrants

to the US last century, there to be translated as – *hopefully*.
After 100 years of standard usage in the US it re-crossed the
Atlantic to Britain where it now firmly resides, although it's
still a much misunderstood orphan.

- **Avoid 'neutralising' adverbs.** Such phrases as *faintly repulsive,
  rather appalling, somewhat threatening* and *slightly lethal* cancel
  out the intended effect. Such an oxymoronic habit should be
  gently stamped out.

Glue (glu) *n.* **1.** any adhesive or sticky substance. – **grammatical glue** *n.* A concept by which verbs, nouns, adjectives, adverbs etc. are stuck together by minor grammatical elements to form sentences.

Grammatical Glue: Determiners, Conjunctions and Prepositions

We have our nouns and pronouns, verbs, adjectives and adjectives – but what now? However much we arrange them they don't seem to make sense, or form proper sentences. Something's missing.

What's missing is the 'grammatical glue' that helps us unite the main action, idea and descriptive words to form clear, cohesive, meaningful statements. This glue consists of relatively small, insignificant words, but don't be fooled. Here are a few of them:

DETERMINERS	*a, the, this, my, which, all*
CONJUNCTIONS	*and, but, or, if, because, like, whereas*
PREPOSITIONS	*with, at, to, for, on, in, around*
INTERJECTIONS	*Ah! Oh! Whew! Wow! Shhh!*

These words and their companions form a mass of grammatical glue with which we construct all our writing and speech. It is simply impossible to communicate without this glue, except perhaps by grunts. If anyone should attempt even a short passage of English without it, the result might look like this:

> *Windows room were wide open, Paris unfolded immense level abyss hollowed itself foot house, built perpendicularly hill. Helene, stretched out long chair, was reading windows.*

It's a bit like listening to particularly bad reception on a radio, or looking at one of those model kits in which all the pieces are present but nothing makes sense until you stick them all together. Here's the paragraph assembled and glued:

> *Both windows of the room were wide open, and Paris unfolded its immense level in the abyss that hollowed itself at the foot of the house, built perpendicularly on the hill. Helene, stretched out on her long chair, was reading at one of the windows.*

Obviously, we should know more about this useful glue.

Determiners

Although they are usually words of fewer than a handful of letters, and mean little or nothing by themselves, **determiners** can help add a lot of information when they precede nouns and noun phrases. They can tell us which particular one or which ones, whose, or how many.

Does that description make determiners sound a bit like adjectives? Well, yes. That's why it's important to know at the outset that while both determiners and adjectives modify nouns and pronouns –

- **Determiners** have very little or no meaning in themselves. What is *the*? Or *my*? Or *which*?

- **Adjectives**, even when they stand alone, convey some meaning. We have a fairly good idea of what the words *black*, *hot*, *crazy*, *lovely* and *clever* mean even when they're not modifying nouns or pronouns.

The two most important determiners are *the*, which is known as the **definite article**, and *a* (or *an* when the attached noun begins with a vowel: *an apple*, *an orchard*), which is called the **indefinite article**. The terms are logical: the definite article *the* is used exclusively to indicate specificity and uniqueness, one of a kind: *the Prime Minister*, *the Archbishop of Canterbury*, *the criminal class*, *the River Thames*. The indefinite article *a* and *an* indicates the general, the non-specific, the collective.

Determiners group themselves under these two headings:

Definite Determiners

DEFINITE ARTICLE	*I will buy **the** car. She will see **the** car.*
POSSESSIVE	*It is now **my** car. He says it's **his** car.*
POSSESSIVE PROPER	*It is **Fred's** car. I say it's **Lynn's** car.*
DEMONSTRATIVE	*I'd like **that** car. He bought **this** car.*
NUMBER	*You have **two** cars? No, just **one** car.*

All these definitive determiners refer to something specific; we are left in no doubt about the identity of the subjects the speaker is referring to. Indefinite determiners, as their name suggests, refer to unspecified, abstract and impersonal entities: *a car* could be one of a million cars.

Indefinite Determiners

INDEFINITE ARTICLE	*I saw **a** great movie. She ate **an** ice cream.*
QUANTIFIER	*She saw **every** movie. I saw **most** movies.*
EXCLAMATORY	***What** a great movie! It was **such** a good movie!*
INTERROGATIVE	***Which** movie? **Whose** ticket did you use?*

Using determiners correctly comes easily during childhood and they rarely give us trouble. We know not to use two determiners together: *I will buy **the a** car. Did you see **some several** movies?* We also learn to drop following nouns: *I saw them **all*** [movies]. *I bought **both*** [cars].

The only source of confusion that arises from using determiners is that many look like pronouns:

DETERMINER	*I find **that** word very confusing.*
PRONOUN	*Do you find **that** confusing?*

Not confusing, really, when you remember that pronouns stand for nouns and stand alone. Determiners always precede the noun they modify.

Conjunctions

Conjunctions are very strong glue because their exclusive purpose in life is to join words and groups of words together:

*Gayle plays the piano **and** the harpsichord.*

In that example, *and* is the conjunction that links two parts of the sentence. It is the simplest kind of conjunction in that it is a link or joiner and nothing more; it adds no new information to the sentence. You could turn it right around without altering the meaning one iota:

*Gayle plays the harpsichord **and** the piano.*

But there are other conjunctions that, while gluing a sentence together, can also impart some extra meaning:

*Gayle likes the piano **but** prefers to play the harpsichord.*

You'll note here that now we have not two, but three items of information: Gayle plays the piano, Gayle plays the harpsichord, Gayle prefers the harpsichord to the piano. The conjunction *but* not only links all this information but supplies an element of exception and contrast.

Here are some other conjunctions, grouped according to the meaning they add to the join:

Expressing	*Some examples*	*Typical usage*
TIME	*before, after, until, till, since, as soon as, while*	*She'll be here **after** dinner.*
PLACE	*where, wherever*	*I'll find out **where** he comes from.*
CAUSE	*because, as, for*	*I feel ill **because** I ate too much.*
CONDITION	*if, although, unless, or, as long as*	*I'll feel better **if** I lie down.*
COMPARISON	*as, than, like, as if, as though*	*It looks **like** it will rain.*
CONTRAST	*although, while, whereas*	*I'm good at English **while** she's best at Maths.*
PURPOSE	*so that, so as to, lest, in order that*	*I must stop **so as to** allow others to speak.*
RESULT	*so, so that, such, that*	*He shouted **so that** they could hear.*

PREFERENCE	*sooner than, rather than*	*I'd eat worms **rather than** go hungry.*
EXCEPTION	*except, except that, excepting that, but*	*He'd play today, **except that** he's torn a muscle.*

It's quite important to know how conjunctions work because they play such a vital part in the construction of well-made sentences. (note the conjunction *because* in that sentence. Would *as* or *for* have worked as well?) So let's analyse the three groups of conjunctions and see how they operate in sentences.

Coordinating Conjunctions. These are so-called because they coordinate units of equal importance, usually units of the same grammatical class:

NOUNS WITH NOUNS	*Daisy planted roses **and** clematis. Will you have tea **or** coffee?*
VERBS WITH VERBS	*The engine coughed **and** slowed to a stop.*
ADJECTIVES WITH ADJECTIVES	*The painting was dark **yet** uplifting.*
ADVERBS WITH ADVERBS	*Slowly **but** surely the tension rose.*
PREPOSITIONAL PHRASES	*Hemingway's 'Across the River **and** into the Trees' is a stirring novel.*
TWO EQUAL IDEAS	*It's my rule never to drink by daylight **and** never to refuse a drink after dark.*

The coordinating conjunctions are *for, and, nor, but, or, yet, so* (there's a mnemonic to help you remember them: *FANBOYS*).

143

Sometimes, for effect, they can start a sentence – but still functioning as conjunctions coordinating two thoughts or ideas:

> *Victoria told me she'd divorce him.* **And** *she did.*
> *He promised he'd pay the money back.* **But** *he didn't.*

At the risk of stating the obvious, conjunctions are usually dropped when there are more than two repeated units to be joined:

> *Neither wind, rain, hail* **nor** *snow will stop him.*
> *They searched for him everywhere: on the continent, in the Caribbean,* **and** *throughout South America without success.*

Subordinating Conjunctions. As the term implies, a subordinating conjunction joins a subordinate unit to the main part of a sentence:

> *They were late* **because** *of the train derailment.*
> *He'll have indigestion* **if** *he eats all that pie.*
> **When** *the food arrives, watch Jim dive in.*

You'll notice that even when you turn these sentences about, the role of the subordinating conjunction remains the same:

> **Because** *of the train derailment, they were late.*
> **If** *he eats all that pie he'll have indigestion.*
> *Watch Jim dive in* **when** *the food arrives.*

You will also see that unlike coordinating conjunctions, which join equal units or thoughts, subordinating conjunctions link unequal units and thoughts. The key point in the first sentence is that they were late; that is a fact. The reason why they were late, in this context, is of secondary importance.

There are quite a few subordinating conjunctions, including *after, although, as, as if, as long as, as soon a*s, *because, before, how, if,* *inasmuch as, in order that, since, so that, than, unless, until, till, when, whereas, whether, while, why.*

Correlative Conjunctions. These are used in pairs to join units or thoughts that have a mutual relationship. And as with coordinating conjunctions, the units they join are of the same grammatical class, nouns and nouns, adverbs and adverbs, and so on:

> **Either** *you go,* **or** *I go.*
> **Neither** *Rick* **nor** *I are prepared to put up with this.*
> *He said that the pair were driving* **not only** *recklessly,* **but also** *without a proper licence.*
> **Both** *Liberals* **and** *Tories are likely to protest.*

Other common correlatives are *either/or, whether/or,* and *whether/if.*

Conjunctions are fairly straightforward although some double as prepositions and can cause confusion. A couple of words in particular need treating with kid gloves: *since* and *like.* Primarily a preposition, *since* expresses an aspect of elapsed time: **Since** *the storm it's rained only once.* It does much the same as an adverb (*She was here last week but we haven't seen her* **since**) and as a conjunction: **Since** *Joe met Sally he hasn't been the same.* The trouble starts when we try to use **since** as a conjunction in place of *because, as* or *for*: **Since** *they knew their MP quite well, they soon got the council's attention.* This usage plainly leads to ambiguity, as we're not sure that they got the council's attention *because* they were friendly with their MP, or only since they got to know him quite well.

The word *like* functions legally as a verb, an adjective, an adverb and as a preposition in various usages. But when it overstretches its versatility to try to be a conjunction it falls flat on its face: *You look* **like** *you've just seen a ghost.* **Like** *I was saying, we'll win tomorrow.* Use genuine conjunctions (*as if* and *as* in those sentences) and you'll stay out of trouble.

GRAMMATICAL GLUE:
Determiners, Conjunctions and Prepositions

Prepositions

About the only thing many of us know about prepositions is that they should never be used to end a sentence *with*! This old rule is mostly ignored these days; instead we are encouraged to use our own judgement on how we should close our sentences. Of greater importance is mastering the subtleties of this energetic, enterprising and indispensable group of words.

A **preposition** usually acts as a joining word, like a conjunction, but it also always adds extra information to the words or sentence elements it links:

> *We went* **to** *the beach.*
> *He rose* **at** *dawn.*
> *She shopped* **for** *some shoes.*

From just these three examples you will have noticed that the prepositions have a particular ability to unite two elements in terms of space (*to*), time (*at*) and reason (*for*). To clarify this important point, here are some of the more common prepositions:

SPACE	*above, between, over, into, near, beside, along, amid*
TIME	*after, at, before, during, since, until, past*
OTHERS	*as, for, in, to, but, by, with, without*
COMPLEX	*instead of, other than, in front of, up to, owing to*

We're familiar with all these common words, even though we may not recognise them as prepositions. Here are a few more that we certainly don't think of as prepositions, but they are: *apropos, bar, circa, cum, minus, notwithstanding, per, plus, pro, qua, re, via* and *vis-à-vis*. Let them be a reminder that prepositions pop up just about everywhere!

Prepositions are especially adept at creating phrases that can function adverbially or adjectivally:

ADVERBIAL PHRASE	*The farmer drove **through the gate**.*
	*She was sitting **in the alcove**.*
	*Eric vanished **with the cash**.*
ADJECTIVAL PHRASE	*He drove along the road **to the farm**.*
	*She sat on the seat **in the alcove**.*
	*Eric was one **of the crooks**.*

In the first three sentences the adverbial phrases are telling us *where* the farmer drove, *where* she sat, and *how* Eric vanished. In each of the other sentences the phrases modify the nouns *road* and *seat* and the pronoun *one*. And to emphasise just how adept prepositions are at creating phrases here's a sentence containing three of them, all functioning as adverbs:

adjective	prep phrase	noun	verb	prep phrase	prep phrase
|	|	|	|	|	|

According **to the movie** *the hero* *fell* **from the cliffs** **into the sea**.

Another interesting thing about prepositions is that when you use one in a sentence, it can be replaced only by another preposition:

> *She found a mouse **in** the house.*
> *She found a mouse **under** the house.*
> *She found a mouse **near** the house.*

. . . and so on. You could substitute any number of prepositions – *beside, inside, behind, beneath* – but only with some difficulty could you substitute any other class of words. It could be said that a preposition is like the keystone of an arch; take it away and . . . you're in trouble!

As with other short versatile words that duck and dive among the grammatical classes, some prepositions can be confused with conjunctions and adverbs:

PREPOSITION   *We had a few drinks **before** dinner.*

CONJUNCTION   *I saw that movie **before** Sarah told me about it.*

ADVERB   *I've seen this movie **before**!*

So, to recap: a **preposition** is followed by its linked noun or noun phrase; a **conjunction** links two elements of a sentence, usually clauses; an **adverb** modifies verbs, adjectives and other adverbs. In the examples above, they all tell us that some event took place previously, but in different ways. As with most of grammar, it's horses for courses.

Another common problem with prepositions is that we tend to create long-winded ones when short ones are freely available. In his *The Complete Plain Words*, Sir Ernest Gowers refers to these as **verbose prepositions**, and gives a list of them together with simpler variants. Here are a few worth avoiding:

Sir Ernest's Verbose Prepositions

*as a consequence of (**because of**)*

*in the course of (**during**)*

*for the purpose of (**to**)*

*in the neighbourhood of (**about**)*

*in addition to (**besides**)*

*in case of (**if**)*

*subsequent to (**after**)*

on the grounds that (**because**)

*in the event of (**if**)*

*in excess of (**more than**)*

*for the reason that (**because**)*

*in the nature of (**like**)*

*with a view to (**to**)*

*prior to (**before**)*

*in order to (**to**)*

Sometimes we're faced with a choice of prepositions and can't decide between them. For example,

Do you	*aim **for***	or	*aim **at**?*
Is it	*disgust **over***	or	*disgust **for**?*
Is it	*superior **than***	or	*superior **to**?*
Are you	*oblivious **to***	or	*oblivious **of**?*

According to the great grammarian Eric Partridge the latter choice in each case represents the correct usage. But this could be disputed, for in many cases the choice can depend on the grammatical construction or the context of the statement. You may *have a dislike for* curry dishes (*dislike* here is a verb) or you may *take a dislike to* curry dishes (*dislike* here is a noun). You may be *possessed of* a sound mind but *possessed **with*** an uncontrollable desire to scream frequently. Here the choice is an idiomatic one because *possessed* is a verb in both cases. An even greater choice challenge is between *admit to* [a crime] and *admit of* [no human failings], both verbs. Fortunately the latter usage, meaning 'leave room for', is now quite rare.

There is, however, general agreement about the following choices:

RECOMMENDED	NOT ADVISED
identical **to**	identical **with**
affinity **between**/**with**	affinity **for**/**to**
inferior **to**	inferior **than**
brood **over**	brood **about**
consequent **on**	consequent **to**
to die **of** [something]	to die **from** [something]
different **from**	different **than**

Idiomatic Prepositions. To those you can add a small collection of common sayings in which the choice of preposition is mostly idiomatic: *an ear **for** music, they'll stop **at** nothing, he's a bit **off** colour, it's all **above** board, it's **beyond** our means, go **with** the flow, go **against** the grain, you'll be **on** call, straight **from** the horse's mouth*.

Using 'onto' and 'on to'. The word *onto* became a preposition by combining *on* and *to*. Once condemned by purists, it is now well established, but that doesn't mean that it is always interchangeable with *on*. *Harry was fined when he drove **onto** the traffic island*, and *Harry was fined when he drove **on** the traffic island* convey two different actions. The first sentence suggests that, accidentally or deliberately, Harry's car mounted the traffic island, and then presumably stopped or drove off again, whereas the second implies that Harry was having a merry time driving around and around on the traffic island. Nor is *onto* interchangeable with *on to*. *When he'd repaired the puncture he drove **on to** his destination. Bill immediately passed the information **on to** the police. Although injured, Zapotek kept right **on to** the finishing line.* In all three cases *on to* is used adverbially and to use the preposition *onto* would be wrong.

The double preposition 'off of'. This double preposition is fairly common, especially in American English. But the *of* is redundant because any sentence written without it loses none of its intended meaning. Thus *He told the boys to get **off of** the grass* should be rewritten as *He told the boys to get **off** the grass*.

Using 'among' and 'between'. Use *between* to connect two persons, objects or ideas: *There is little difference **between** the two of them. She couldn't tell the difference **between** either of them.* *Among* is used in connection with several entities: *There is little difference **among** all five candidates. He shared the reward **among** his friends.* However, where several things are considered individually, *between* might be a better choice: *He divided the reward equally **between** the five of us.* It's also worth remembering that when describing a choice, *between* is followed by *and*, not *or*: *It's a matter of choosing between Jane **and** George* (not *Jane **or** George*). And although *amongst* is still widely used, discriminating writers prefer *among*.

Using 'round' for the preposition 'around'. *The lady looked **round**,* or, *The lady looked **around**?* In the unintentionally comic first example there is a temptation to substitute *around*, but that would be a departure from standard British usage; in British English *round* used prepositionally is a linguistic fixture, while *around* is standard in American English. It is now accepted that they are interchangeable, the choice depending on euphony, but the use of *around* to mean 'approximately' is still frowned upon: *They collected around £60 for the fund.* Use *about*.

Ending sentences with prepositions. Once the biggest prepositional bogey of them all, today the argument about ending sentences with prepositions hardly merits serious comment. The reason for the objection can be traced back to the influence of Latin grammar on English; in Latin, ending a sentence with a preposition was a non-starter. Generations of scholars upheld the rule, although when such masters of the language as Shakespeare (in *Hamlet*: 'No traveller returns, puzzles the will, / And makes us rather bear those ills we have / Than fly to others that we know not of?') used them unapologetically, a rethink on the positioning of prepositions began. The view today is that unless a prepositional ending sends jarring notes to the ear (*I think we'll find that sour wine is what that barrel is probably full of*), let it stay. A sentence such as *That's the restaurant we ate in* is perfectly acceptable to all but a few pedants. Quite often, extremely clumsy sentences will result from straining to avoid finishing with a preposition – a practice famously lampooned by Winston Churchill when, criticising a civil servant's prose, he commented: 'This is the sort of English *up* with which I shall not put'.

One final but growing problem with prepositions is that the lazier among us tend to drop them altogether: *Defenestration means throwing someone out the window* should of course read *out **of** the window*. It is a habit to be discouraged.

Interjections!

These are exclamatory expressions used to add force and meaning to our speech and writing. Some have been converted from existing words (*Look out! Oh dear! Cheers!*); some have been converted to verbs (to *pooh-pooh*, to *shoo*, to *boo*) or nouns (*boos*, a *boo-boo*). As a family of words – if they are a family – they resist being governed by any rules, except perhaps those of taste. A few examples:

> *Ah! Aaaah. . . Aha! Oh! Ooh! Eh? Shhh! Ouch! Pwawh!*
> *Gee! Ha-ha! Ha-ha-ha Te-he-he Hey! Oops! mmm . . .*
> *Phew! Wow! Yuk! Whoops! uh-uh tsk tut-tut psst . . .*
> *Gosh! Blimey! Cheers! Damn! Ugh! Gordon Bennett!*

Grammatical Gluemanship: a Two Minute Test

Here's a two-minute test to check your connections. Answer **A** or **B**. The answers are at the end of this chapter.

1.   One is an adverb, the other a preposition. In which sentence is the preposition used correctly:

   A   *She loved to walk besides the lake.*

   B   *She loved to walk beside the lake.*

2.   There's a mismatched pair of correlative conjunctions here. Which is correct?

   A   *Roy said he liked neither the soup nor the main course.*

   B   *Roy said he liked neither the soup or the main course.*

3.   What's wrong here? Choose the grammatically correct sentence.

   A   *The boy sang like his life depended on it.*

   B   *The boy sang as if his life depended on it.*

4.   Which sentence conveys a clear picture of the action?

   A   *Bring your book into the conservatory where it's more comfortable.*

   B   *Bring your book in the conservatory where it's more comfortable.*

5.   Grammatically correct sentences are always more elegant. Which one?

   A *The crisis came just after Mrs Hale called the doctor.*

   B *The crisis was just after Mrs Hale called the doctor.*

6.   Strictly speaking, both sentences are correct. But which is "more correct" than the other?

   A *Sheila got her handbag off of a market stall.*

   B *Sheila got her handbag off a market stall.*

7. Between you and me and the gatepost, something's wrong with one of these sentences. Which is correct?

   A *The chief ordered the booty to be split between the whole tribe.*

   B *The chief ordered the booty to be split among the whole tribe.*

8. Keeping in mind how correlative conjunctions work, pick which of these sentences uses a pair correctly.

   A *The meal was not only a disaster, but also a wasted evening.*

   B *The meal was not only a disaster, but a wasted evening, too.*

9. Pick the appropriate preposition:

   A *The conditions were quite different than what he was used to.*

   B *The conditions were quite different from what he was used to.*

10. A preposition too many, or one too few? Which is correct?

    A *The cat ran out of the door and disappeared.*

    B *The cat ran out the door and disappeared.*

Answers

1. **B** *Besides* is an adverb; *beside* is the preposition.   2. **A** *Neither/nor* is the matching correlative.   3. **B** *Like* is a verb and adjective and shouldn't be used as a conjunction. *As though* or *as if* would be correct.   4. **A** *Into*, not *in*.   5. **A** *Came* is correct in this context. 6. **B** The *of* part of the double preposition is redundant.   7. **B** Use *among* when the object consists of more than two people or things. 8. **A** The correct correlative pair is *not only/but also*.   9. **B** Different *from*, not different *than*.   10. **A** In sentence **B**, the preposition *of* is missing.

Scoring. Achieving a score of ten shouldn't be too difficult. Any score of less than seven points would suggest that you seek better connections.

PUNCTUATION:
What's the Point?

The dots, strokes and squiggles may appear physically insignificant on a page of print and evanescent in our speech, but without them all would be chaos. Not knowing how to use them correctly can result in even greater chaos. If you were to say to someone:

I hate habitual liars; like you, I find them detestable.

that person would very likely agree. But imagine the reaction should you monkey slightly with the punctuation:

I hate habitual liars like you; I find them detestable.

Old-time teachers were fond of quoting this chestnut: *KING CHARLES I PRAYED HALF AN HOUR AFTER HE WAS BEHEADED.* A stop in the right place (between *PRAYED* and *HALF*) returns the statement to history as we know it. Another well-known illustration recounts the fate of a warrior in ancient Greece who, on the eve of leaving for a war, consulted the Oracle at Delphi. *Thou shalt go thou shalt return never by war shalt thou perish*, he was told. The overworked Oracle spoke without pause, so the warrior naturally assumed that he meant *Thou shalt go, thou shalt return, never by war shalt thou perish* and departed with great confidence. Unfortunately he was killed in the first battle, never realising that what the Oracle really meant was, *Thou shalt go, thou shalt return never, by war shalt thou perish*.

Less morbid are those grammatical gags and puzzles based on the omission of commas and other marks: *The farmer raised sheep dogs and pigs* (*The farmer raised sheep, dogs and pigs*); *What is is what is not is not is it not* (*What is, is; what is not, is not; is it not?*). You can clearly see that we need punctuation to help us express and make clear on paper what is intuitively easy with speech.

Two centuries ago, most punctuation took its cues from speech. This was a period when the predominant practice of reading aloud, with its pauses and dramatic stresses, was translated into written punctuation – rhetorical punctuation.

A hundred years on, with increased literacy, the spoken word gave way to the written. The emphasis now was on meaning rather than dramatic effect, and rhetorical (or oratorical) punctuation bowed to a more logical system. Today we have a blend of both: a system capable of conveying force, intonation, urgency, tension, doubt, rhythm and passion while never abandoning its duty to consistency and clarity of meaning.

Punctuation probably reached its zenith in the late 19th century, helping to make sense of the then fashionably interminable sentences. Sentences held together by a dozen or more commas, semi-colons, brackets and other marks were commonplace. Nowadays sentences, influenced by the brevity of newspaper style, are shorter, and the need for the complicated division within long sentences has all but disappeared. Commas are freely dropped where the meaning remains unaffected. Stops after abbreviations are disappearing in a general quest for typographic tidiness. The majority of the English-speaking population probably goes through life without ever using, on paper, any punctuation marks other than the comma, dash and full stop.

Don't, however, be led astray by this tolerance. While parsimony in punctuation may be adequate for the majority, it will be of little use to you if you wish to raise your standards of communication. The role of punctuation in writing good English cannot be underestimated.

The marks that help us punctuate our writing can be divided into three groups:

- **UNITS OF SPACE:** Sentences and paragraphs.

- **DEVICES FOR SEPARATING AND JOINING:** Full stops, commas, semi-colons, colons, brackets, dashes and hyphens.

- **SYMBOLS OF MEANING:** Question and exclamation marks, quotation marks, apostrophes, strokes, asterisks, bullets, italics and underlining.

Units of Space are a basic form of punctuation. They separate words, sentences and paragraphs and have already been discussed in the chapter *Let's Look at Sentences* (page 25). Now let us look at the remaining two groups.

Punctuation: Devices for Separating and Joining

*Sentences begin with a Capital letter / To help you make your writing
better / Use full stops to mark the end / Of every sentence you have penned.*
So runs the old schoolteachers' rhyme, and although it seems
absurdly basic you'd be surprised by the number of people who
either use full stops where they shouldn't or neglect to use them
where they should.

The Full Stop

'Punctuation', *The Times* advises its journalists, 'is . . . not a
fireworks display to show off your dashes and gaspers. Remember
the first rule: the best punctuation is the full stop.'

The **full stop** (or stop, point or period) is the most emphatic,
abrupt and unambiguous of all the punctuation marks. It is used
like a knife to cut off a sentence at the required length. The rule is

that simple: where you place your stop is up to you, but generally it is at the point where a thought is complete. When you are about to embark on another thought, that's the time to think about a full stop. Master this principle and you can then move on to using full stops stylistically, for emphasis:

> *You couldn't get near Harry all day because he was*
> *constantly on the prowl, hunched in his greasy pants and*
> *dirty sweater, looking mean and taciturn and with his mind*
> *no doubt churning with murderous thoughts, for he had*
> *announced to too many people in too many places and in too*
> *loud a voice that he would kill Evans the instant he clapped*
> *eyes on him. And he did.*

That delayed full stop, preceded by mounting tension and followed by the shock conclusion delivered in just three words, helps to convey an almost casual callousness. The two stops serve their purpose perfectly; they make the reader stop and reflect. Here's another passage, this time displaying a variety of punctuation marks. The full stop, however, is easily the most predominant:

> *With intense frustration, Giles grabbed the man, surprising*
> *him.*
> *'No you don't!' he yelled hoarsely.*
> *The man recovered, fighting back. Fiercely. Savagely.*
> *Hard breathing. Curses. Grunts. The wincing thud of fists.*
> *An alarming stream of crimson from Giles's left eye.*
> *Pulses racing, they glared at one another, each daring the other*
> *to make a move. A car horn in the distance. Shouts.*

That's highly stylised prose, and could be criticised for its over-use of sentence fragments rather than complete sentences. But here the heavy-handed application of the full stop is deliberate, for we can see what the writer is getting at – capturing the harsh punch-punch-punch of a ferocious fist fight.

At the other extreme many writers try to project a stream-of-consciousness effect by chucking out all punctuation, including full stops. One famous example is a passage in James Joyce's *Ulysses* which goes on and on for over a thousand words without so much as a pause. But the author did need a full stop at the end!

Full stops control the length of your sentences, so remember:

- Try to keep sentences variable in length, but generally short.

- Using long sentences doesn't necessarily make you a better writer.

- To use *only* full stops is as unnatural as walking without using your knee and ankle joints. Consider the use of other punctuation marks.

The Comma

The **comma** is the most flexible and most versatile of all the punctuation marks. And because it is also the least emphatic mark it is also the most complex and subtle. Not surprisingly, many writers feel a nagging uncertainty about using commas.

A lot of the trouble with commas arises because many people seem to think of them as indicating 'breath pauses'. That may have been the case when the language was more orally inclined, and in much early prose it is common to find commas following speech patterns. Today, however, the placement of commas invariably follows grammatical logic rather than to indicate rhetorical pauses:

> *Every year over the British Isles, half a million meteorites enter the atmosphere.*

You can hear the lecturer intoning that, can't you – with a dramatic pause before announcing 'half a million meteorites enter the atmosphere.' Try it. But when you write it as a sentence you'll find that the comma is redundant:

> *Every year over the British Isles half a million meteorites enter the atmosphere.*

Even so, wrong comma placement is exceedingly common. Here's a typical offender in the *Economist*: 'But the ferry's high cost and steadily declining number of passengers, cannot be cured by government subsidy.' Such a sentence needs no commas at all.

Most writing today requires commas that serve a logical purpose, usually to separate different thoughts or nuances of thought within sentences:

> *The snapshot with its naively honest images revolutionised our way of seeing the world.*

Because this sentence would make essentially the same statement if it were written as *The snapshot revolutionised our way of seeing the world*, the incidental clause *with its naively honest images* is a relevant but separate thought, and should be separated from the main thrust of the statement by commas:

> *The snapshot, with its naively honest images, revolutionised our way of seeing the world.*

You'll notice that two commas are required for this job; a common mistake is to omit the second enclosing comma.

Functions of the Comma

SETTING APART NAMES AND PERSONS

> *Are you meeting him tomorrow, John?*
> *Listen, Joyce, I've had enough.*
> *And that, ladies and gentlemen, is that.*

ITEMISING WORDS	*Please place all towels, costumes, clothing and valuables in the lockers provided.*
ITEMISING WORD GROUPS	*Please place any articles of clothing, swimming and sporting equipment, personal belongings, but not money and jewellery, in the lockers.*
ENCLOSING ADDITIONAL THOUGHTS OR QUALIFICATIONS	*The occasion was, on the whole, conducted with considerable dignity. The judges thought it was, arguably, one of his finest novels.*
SETTING APART INTERJECTIONS	*Look, I've had enough! Blimey, isn't the beach crowded!*
BEFORE DIRECT SPEECH	*Jill turned abruptly and said, 'If that's the way you feel, then go home!'*
INTRODUCING QUESTIONS	*You'll be going soon, won't you? She's marrying James tomorrow, isn't she?*
EMPHASISING POINTS OF VIEW	*Naturally, I'll look after the car. Of course, she fully deserves it.*
SETTING OFF COMPARATIVE OR CONTRASTING STATEMENTS	*The taller they are, the farther they fall. The more he said he adored Maisie, the less she cared.*
REINFORCING STATEMENTS	*She's ill because she won't eat, that's why! It'll come right in the end, I'm sure.*

AFTER INTRODUCTORY WORDS

Sausages, which are far from fat free, pose a problem for dieters

Omitting the opening comma required to separate a subordinate clause (*which are far from fat free*) from the main clause (*Sausages . . . pose a problem for dieters*) is a common mistake, and one that usually leads to ambiguity. With the commas correctly in place, as in our example, we are in no doubt that the description 'far from fat free' applies to all sausages. But omit that opening comma and a different meaning can be conveyed: *Sausages which are far from fat free, pose a problem for dieters*.

Now the statement is saying that only those sausages that are 'far from fat free' are a problem. But if that is what is actually meant, the remaining comma is redundant.

Here's another example, from *The Times*:

Overnight fans had painted messages on the road outside his home . . . 'We love you Frank'.

Overnight fans? Are these a different breed from ordinary fans? Obviously a comma after the separate thought 'Overnight' is required to make things clear.

Using commas appropriately also includes not *over-using* them:

It is, curiously, surprising when, say, you hear your name announced in a foreign language, or even in a strange accent.

Although grammatically correct that sentence seems to be hedged with *ifs, buts, maybes* and pontifications. Can it be rewritten in a more direct style, while still conveying the several shades of meaning?

Curiously, it is surprising when, for example, you hear your

163

*name announced in a foreign language or even in a strange
accent.*

The sentence, less two commas, is now a little more direct.
Here's another example of 'comma bloat' which can be rewritten
without using any commas at all.

*Mr Burkitt had not, previously, met the plaintiff, except
when, in 1974, he had, unexpectedly, found himself in Paris.*

It's worth looking a little closer at comma-reduction. Take
this simple sentence:

A   *My hobby, trainspotting, is, to many, a bit of a joke.*
B   *My hobby, trainspotting, is to many, a bit of a joke.*
C   *My hobby, trainspotting, is to many a bit of a joke.*
D   *My hobby trainspotting, is to many a bit of a joke.*
E   *My hobby trainspotting is to many a bit of a joke.*

Pedants might claim that all these sentences differ in
nuances of meaning, but to the average reader they all mean the
same thing. So we are left with choosing which one we would use
to express our thought clearly, economically and elegantly. Which
version would you choose? (Our choice would be **C**, but it is our
personal preference and not one we would wish to impose on
others).

To some extent the apt use of commas is an acquired skill –
but certainly one worth pursuing. Merely scanning a sentence for
sense and clarity will usually tell you. The writer of the following
sentence was either afraid of commas or intent on speed of delivery:

The land is I believe owned by the City Council.

Most of us would place commas after *is* and *believe*, because the phrase 'I believe' is an important qualifier and needs to be highlighted from the main statement, *The land is . . . owned by the City Council* which, by itself, may or may not be true.

The 'comma splice'

Another common comma error is the so-called **comma splice** – the use of a comma in place of a linking word to unite two sentences in the mistaken belief that it will form a single sentence:

> *The house is large, it has seven bedrooms.*

That is not a grammatical sentence, but there are several ways to make it one:

> *The house is large; it has seven bedrooms.*
> *The house is large because it has seven bedrooms.*
> *The house is large and includes seven bedrooms.*
> *The house is large, with seven bedrooms.*

Using Commas with Adjectives

See if you can work out, in these two sentences, why one has the adjectives separated by commas, and the other does not:

> *The night resounded with a loud, chilling, persistent ringing.*
> *It was a large brick Victorian mansion.*

The reasons are embodied in two seemingly simple rules worth remembering:

- Where the adjectives (or other modifiers) define <u>separate</u> attributes (*loud, chilling, persistent*), they are best separated by commas.

- Where the adjectives work together to create a

<u>single</u> image (*large, brick, Victorian*), the commas are best omitted.

Two seemingly simple rules, but they can be tricky to apply. Sometimes you may be led into ambiguity, and have to resort to common sense:

Myra was a pretty smart young woman.
Myra was a pretty, smart young woman.

Well, does the writer mean that Myra was pretty *and* smart, or just very smart?

The Oxford, or Final Comma

The Times advises its journalists to 'avoid the so-called Oxford comma: *x, y and z* and not *x, y, and z*'. What this means is that:

Martin spoke to Edith, Lesley, Bunty and Samantha.

is preferred to

Martin spoke to Edith, Lesley, Bunty, and Samantha.

Sound advice; a final comma before *and* in a list is now outmoded – unless there is the possibility of ambiguity:

The colours of the flag are red, green and gold in stripes.

What does this mean? Red and green, with gold stripes? Red, green and gold stripes? Red, with green and gold stripes? What the sentence needs is a comma for clarity. If, as intended, the statement was meant to describe a flag consisting of just three bold stripes, it should say so: *The colours of the flag are red, green, and gold, in stripes.*

Other Problem Comma Placements

Sometimes you will find that verbs will need enclosing by commas to help guide readers through a complex passage:

In the daytime, **sleeping***, the baby was adorable, but at nights,* **howling continuously***, she was a tyrant and a monster.*

Few writers would attempt that kind of construction with the prospect of wrestling with such complex comma placements. But a very common sentence construction is frequently marred by confusion about where to insert a comma:

Jeremy glanced at the clock, and abruptly closing his book, leapt up from the sofa.

There's something vaguely amiss with this, isn't there? What's amiss is that the comma should follow the *and*, not precede it. Again, we must separate the two structural components of the sentence, the main clause (*Jeremy glanced at the clock and . . leapt up from the sofa*) and a subordinate clause (*abruptly closing his book*) to discover where the *and* really belongs. When we find it belongs to the main clause we can place the comma in the correct position. So the sentence should read:

Jeremy glanced at the clock and, abruptly closing his book, leapt up from the sofa.

or

Jeremy glanced at the clock, and, abruptly closing his book, leapt up from the sofa.

Using Commas to Parenthesise

One of the most interesting, but also perhaps the most

167

contentious, use of commas, is to parenthesise (or bracket) relevant but not essential matter from the main part of the sentence:

> *The wild hyacinths (which are now at the height of their season) tint the woods with a pale blue mist.*

The essential message here is *The wild hyacinths tint the woods with a pale blue mist.* But then we've had a further thought – *which are now at the height of their season* – which we'd like to include in the same sentence. Sometimes we enclose such additions in parenthesis (brackets) as above, but mostly we use a pair of far more convenient and less disruptive commas:

> *The wild hyacinths, which are now at the height of their season, tint the woods with a pale blue mist.*

Now that we've seen how commas are used to isolate subordinate statements, what are these two commas doing in this sentence?

> *The two lead actors, who appear in 'Grease', won their respective roles after many gruelling years in musicals.*

The two enclosing commas here are telling us that *who appear in 'Grease'* is non-essential information. But if you rewrite the sentence without that phrase it doesn't make sense: we don't know who the lead actors are or what they are doing.

In fact *who appear in 'Grease'* is a defining or restrictive phrase – one that identifies, modifies or qualifies its subject. It is essential, not non-essential, information. So the sentence should read:

> *The two lead actors who appear in 'Grease' won their respective roles after many gruelling years in musicals.*

To summarise:

- Where a phrase or clause does not define or qualify the subject, indicate that it is non-essential matter by isolating it with a pair of commas.

- Where a phrase or clause defines or qualifies the subject, weld it to the subject by omitting the commas.

The Semicolon

There is something about semicolons that can raise the blood pressure. The writer George Orwell was so against them that he wrote one of his novels, *Coming Up For Air* (1939), without a single semicolon in it. Actually, three crept in, only to be removed in later editions. George Bernard Shaw complained of T E Lawrence that while he threw colons about like a madman he hardly used semicolons at all. More recently Martin Amis, in his novel *Money*, reportedly used just one. Indeed, the heat provoked by the anti-semicolonists some years ago led to fears that the mark would become an endangered species, and a Society for the Preservation of the Semicolon was formed.

A **semicolon** is a pause somewhere between a strong comma and a weak full stop. And despite its dismissal by many writers and teachers it has a number of practical grammatical and stylistic functions:

- **To join words, word groups and sentences.** Occasionally we find ourselves writing a long sentence with too many connecting words such as *and*, *but* and *also*, with the danger of getting into an impossible tangle:

  > *The history of the semicolon and colon is one of confusion because there are no precise rules governing their use and, furthermore, many writers would argue that both marks are*

*really stylistic rather than parenthetical devices, and can in
any case be easily replaced by commas, stops and dashes, and
there the argument rests.*

There's nothing grammatically wrong with that but it is
unwieldy and unappealing to both eye and mind. Many writers
would, without hesitation, recast it as two or more separate
sentences:

*The history of the semicolon and colon is one of confusion.
There are no precise rules governing their use. Many writers
argue that both marks are really stylistic rather than
parenthetical devices which can easily be replaced by
commas, stops and dashes. And there the argument rests.*

We have previously seen how the judicious use of full stops
to achieve shorter sentences can aid understanding, and that is
certainly the case here. But some writers, feeling that the original
long sentence is, after all, about a single subject and should
therefore be kept as a whole and not split apart, would turn to the
semicolon to achieve unity of thought without making things hard
for the reader:

*The history of the semicolon and colon is one of confusion;
there are no precise rules governing their use; many writers
argue that both marks are really stylistic rather than
parenthetical devices and that they can easily be replaced by
commas, stops and dashes; and there the argument rests.*

● **To separate word groups already containing commas.** Any
sentence that is essentially a list should be crystal clear and easily
read. Most 'sentence lists' adequately separate the items with
commas, but sometimes the items themselves are groups
containing commas and require semicolons for clarity. These two
examples illustrate just how handy semicolons can be:

> *Those present included Mr and Mrs Allison, their daughters*
> *Sarah, Megan and Sue; the Smith twins; Reg and Paul*
> *Watson; Joyce, Helen and Bill Hobson; etc.*
> *The line-up consisted of Bix Beiderbecke, cornet; Al Grande,*
> *trombone; George Johnson, tenor sax; Bob Gillette, banjo;*
> *Dick Voynow, piano, and Vic Moore on drums.*

● **To restore order to sentences suffering from 'Comma Riot'.**
Here's a longish but reasonably accomplished sentence spoiled by
'comma riot':

> *His main aims in life, according to Wilma, were to achieve*
> *financial independence, to be powerfully attractive, not only*
> *to women but in particular to rich ladies, to eat and drink*
> *freely without putting on weight, to remain fit, vital and*
> *young-looking beyond his eightieth birthday and, last but not*
> *least, to not only read, but fully understand, Professor*
> *Stephen Hawking's 'A Brief History of Time'.*

Many professional writers would defend this sentence,
despite its eleven commas. But others, perhaps more concerned
with clarity than rhythm, would suggest that some of the thoughts
at least should be separated by the longer pauses provided by
semicolons:

> *His main aims in life, according to Wilma, were to achieve*
> *financial independence; to be powerfully attractive, not only*
> *to women but in particular to rich ladies; to eat and drink*
> *freely without putting on weight; to remain fit, vital and*
> *young-looking beyond his eightieth birthday and, last but not*
> *least, to not only read but fully understand Professor Stephen*
> *Hawking's 'A Brief History of Time'.*

● **To provide pauses before certain adverbs.** There are certain
adverbs and conjunctions that require a preceding pause, but one
longer and stronger than that provided by a comma. Look at this
example:

WITH A COMMA *It was a beautiful car, moreover it was economical to run.*

WITH A SEMICOLON *It was a beautiful car; moreover it was economical to run.*

You can see and *hear* that need for a substantial pause before *moreover*, can't you?

A comma is wrong on both grammatical and rhetorical counts. Here's another example; read it and note your instinctive pause before *nevertheless*:

> *Joe claimed he'd beaten the bookies on every race; nevertheless he was broke as usual when he left the track.*

Watch out for *therefore, however, besides, also, moreover, furthermore, hence, consequently* and *subsequently*; in many constructions they will require a preceding semicolon.

● **To induce a mild shock or make a joke.** Semicolons can help the writer emphasise contrast and incongruity. For a woman to remark,

> *I thought his wife was lovely but that her dress was in poor taste.*

would be fairly pedestrian and certainly lacking in feminine acuity. Here's what she might wish she'd said with the tart use of a mental semicolon:

> *I loved his wife; pity about the frock.*

A semicolon is adroitly used by Henry Thoreau in *Walden*, although in a more self-deprecating vein:

> *I had more visitors while I lived in the woods than at any other period in my life; I mean that I had some.*

172

The Colon

The legendary grammarian Henry Fowler defined the function of the **colon** as 'delivering the goods that have been invoiced in the preceding words'. More matter-of-factly, the colon acts as a pointing finger, as if to warn the reader about a statement ahead: 'Wait for it . . . here it comes!'

Although under threat from the dash, the colon is a versatile workhorse, and many colon-scoffers are silenced when confronted with the range of its functions:

● **To introduce a list.** This is probably how colons are most commonly used:

> *Detective Stevens entered and took it all in: the body, the still smouldering mattress, the cigarette butts on the floor . . .*

● **To present a conclusion.**

> *There was one very obvious reason for Ernest's failure to keep the job: his right hand never knew what his left was doing.*

● **To present an explanation or example.**

> *There are three reasons why Lainston House near Winchester is an outstanding restaurant: excellent cuisine, beautifully restored interiors, and super-attentive staff.*

● **To introduce a quotation or indirect speech.**

> *Gradually, one by one, the words came back to me: 'And we forget because we must and not because we will.'*
> *The Mayor strode to the platform, opened his notes and glared at the assembly: 'You have not come here for nothing,' he growled.*

● **As a substitute for a conjunction.** In this example, the writer preferred the punchier colon to a choice of conjunctions such as *and* or *but*:

> *Rodriguez felled him with a dazzling left hook that came out of nowhere: Hayman did not get up.*

● **To introduce questions.**

> *The essential issue is simply this: did she or did she not seduce Sir Timothy in the stable block?*

● **To introduce subtitles.**

> *Gilbert White: Observer in God's Little Acre.*
> *Men at War: An Introduction to Chess.*

● **To link contrasting statements.** In this role the colon shares with the semicolon the ability to administer surprise and shock. The choice is a matter of taste:

> *Her love affair with her son's school, its history, its achievements, its famous alumni and its crumbling charm would have endured for ever but for one minor consideration: the £12,000 yearly fees.*

It's worth remembering that:

- The difference between a colon and a semicolon is not a difference in weight or force; the two marks are mostly used for quite different purposes.

- A colon is never followed by a capital letter, except with proper nouns: *Emma, Ford Motor Co*, etc.

- Don't use colons where they are not needed, as in: *The man was amazing, and was able to play: the piano,*

violin, double bass, trombone, clarinet, harp and drums.
The colon is clearly redundant.

Brackets and Parentheses

In our discussion of commas we saw how material could be set apart or parenthesised (the term *parenthesis*, via Latin and Greek, means 'an insertion besides') by enclosing it between two commas.

The sentence above is just such an example, except that instead of using a pair of commas we have used a pair of **brackets** or, more correctly, **parentheses** or round ( ) brackets. The function of square brackets is discussed later.

If you look at that first sentence again, you will see that the brackets serve to set apart relevant matter which could, if you wished to be ruthless, be dropped altogether.

The bracket's embrace is seductive and extremely adaptable, as the following catalogue of examples of usage will demonstrate:

ADDING INFORMATION
One of the earliest dictionaries is that of Elisha Coles (London, 1685).

OFFERING EXPLANATION
Unable to follow the instructions in French and after nothing but trouble she returned the car (a Renault saloon) to the garage.

AFTERTHOUGHT
Travel by car, choose the cross-channel route that offers best value for money, and look out for bargains (like newspaper tokens. Last summer we scored a free hotel in France).

CLARIFICATION
The directive stated quite clearly (page 394, second paragraph) that the department would be closed from March 1.

COMMENT	*Cruelty to animals (I noted a scene in which a donkey's tail was tied to a post, and another where a tin can with a lit firecracker in it was attached to a dog's tail) was a fairly common sight in children's comic papers in the 1920s.*
ILLUSTRATION	*The candidate spent far too long discussing irrelevancies (20 minutes on the price of footwear; another ten on tax havens) with the inevitable result that most of us walked out.*
TO EXPRESS AN ASIDE	*She claims to be thirty-five (and pigs can fly).*
TO INDICATE OPTIONS	*Your document(s) will be returned in due course.*

There is an important grammatical difference between parenthesising material within commas and within brackets. Generally, material enclosed by commas is still very much part of the sentence, and should observe the grammatical conventions of that sentence. Bracketed material, on the other hand, is rather more distanced from the sentence into which it is inserted, and can assume its own punctuation.

The Square Bracket

The square bracket has an entirely different function from that of parentheses: words enclosed within them are not intended to be part of a sentence, but as an editorial or authorial interjection:

It was a matter of opinion that if offered the position, he [Professor Brandmeyer] would most likely refuse it on moral grounds.

That sentence came at the end of a very long paragraph; the professor's name had been mentioned at the beginning, but other names and much discussion followed so that the late reference to *he* was in danger of being misunderstood. The editor therefore inserted the name [*Professor Brandmeyer*] in square brackets as a reminder and also to indicate that the intervention was the editor's and not the author's.

One of the most common uses of square brackets is to enclose the adverb *sic* (from the Latin *sicut*, meaning 'just as') to indicate that incorrect or doubtful matter is quoted exactly from the original:

> *Pink and yellow concubines [sic] climbed in great profusion up the trellis.*
>
> *Miss Patricia Wall Wall [sic] with her fiancé Mr Gerald Kleeman.*

The second example was a caption under a photograph of the newly engaged couple; *The Times* wanted to make sure that readers understood that 'Wall Wall' really was the young lady's surname and not a misprint.

The Dash

Although the dash is a much maligned mark – especially by punctuation purists who decry its substitution for the colon – it has in recent times attracted a growing band of defenders. 'It's the most exciting and dramatic punctuation mark of them all!' claim some.

Primarily used to interrupt or extend a sentence, the dash is an extraordinarily versatile mark when used creatively. It is a bit of a larrikin with a disdain for rules and thus can be a lot of fun in the often po-faced world of punctuation. But here are some of the more respectable ways in which the dash will be found useful:

LINKING DEVICE	*Mrs Sims had four daughters – Poppy, Iris, Pansy and Petal.*
AS A PAUSE	*Everyone expected the poet to be controversial – but not to the extent of swearing at the chairwoman and falling off the stage.*
CUEING A SURPRISE	*The adhesive gave way, the beard came adrift and Santa Claus was revealed as – Aunt Clara!*
NOTING AN EXCEPTION	*A straight line is the shortest distance between two points – when you're sober.*
INDICATING HESITATION	*'There will be, of course, er– a small charge, because – well, er – '*
SEPARATING LISTS	*She assembled all the ingredients – flour, sugar, eggs, salt, lard and raisins – and started on the pudding.*
AFTERTHOUGHTS	*They babbled on, delighted at sighting the rare parakeet – I didn't see so much as a feather.*

Where the dash is used parenthetically – to enclose matter in much the same way as with brackets or commas – don't forget the second dash. It's an omission which trips many people – even the grammar authority G V Carey in his *Mind The Stop* (1939):

> *No wonder that in some matters the dash has fallen into disrepute; but I still maintain that, if kept in its place – and I make one here for luck, it is a very useful stop.*

The sentence calls for a dash, not a comma, after *luck*. It's a lesson to us all – not to be slapdash with the dash!

The Hyphen

Although both are little horizontal lines – albeit one a shade shorter than the other – hyphens and dashes are not related. A hyphen joins two or more words together, while a dash keeps them apart. What they do have in common is that they are inclined to be overused and abused.

The rules governing the use of hyphens, such as they are, are about the most contradictory and volatile in grammar. And yet their purpose is simple: to help us construct words to clarify meaning and avoid ambiguity. Take these two similar newspaper headlines:

> *MAN EATING TIGER SEEN NEAR MOTORWAY.*
> *MAN-EATING TIGER SEEN NEAR MOTORWAY.*

The first headline suggests that a hungry gourmet has decided to barbecue some choice jungle beast near a motorway, while the second could prove fatal should you be carelessly wandering along the hard shoulder. A hyphen has made all the difference.

Hyphens enable us to create useful compounds by uniting two or more associated words. Sometimes the marriage is permanent. A *book seller* became a *book-seller* and is now a *bookseller*. *Life* got engaged to *like* to become *life-like*; they are now commonly married as *lifelike*. Many other common words began their careers as two separate words before being temporarily linked by hyphens: *earring, lampshade, postgraduate, prehistoric, seaside, today, washbowl*.

Many hyphenated couplings exist primarily to obviate confusion. Have you ever seen a stick walking? Or shuddered at an ear splitting, or witnessed a room changing? Obviously not, but just in case of a misunderstanding we hyphenate: *walking-stick, ear-splitting, changing-room*.

179

Then there are hyphenated couples never destined to become permanent partners because of 'letter collision' which is visually disconcerting: *shell-like* (not *shelllike*); *semi-illiterate* (not *semiilliterate*); *de-ice* (not *deice*); *co-wrote* (not *cowrote*) – although we accept such unhyphenated words as *cooperative* and *coordination*.

Generally, hyphens are used after the prefixes *ex-* (ex-cop); *non-* (non-starter) and *self-* (self-employed). They are not usually required after *anti-* (antifreeze); *counter-* (counterweight); *co-* (coreligionist); *neo-* (neoclassicism); *pre-* (prehensile); and *un-* (unconditional). But there are some exceptions: *co-respondent* (to distinguish it from a misspelt *correspondent*!) and *re-creation* (not *recreation*).

Wordbreaks and Linebreaks

Aside from helping to construct compound words, hyphens enable us to split words at the end of lines. Normally, words are split according to **syllabication** (or syl-lab-i-ca-tion) which follows the logic of word construction. But it is apparent that a lot of modern typesetting follows no such rules and words are likely to be split on rather more *laissez-faire* principles, giving rise to such unlikely compounds as *fig-urine, the-ories, should-er, condom-inium, physiothe-rapists, hor-semen*, and *mans-laughter*.

Hassle-free Hyphenating

Unfortunately the business of hyphenating is never likely to be completely hassle-free. The reason is that hyphenated and unhyphenated compound words are being created all the time and it can take a decade before there is anything like universal agreement on the final fixed form of a word. Most professional writers, while conscientious about hyphen correctness, take the advice of Sir Ernest Gowers who, in his *The Complete Plain Words*, wrote, 'If you take hyphens seriously you will surely go mad'.

Meanwhile here is a guide to many hyphenated words and names likely to crop up in everyday usage:

accident-prone, acid-free, anti-abortion, attorney-at-law, awe-inspiring

bird-brain, bleary-eyed, bone-shaking, bull's-eye, brother-in-law

call-up, cat-o'-nine-tails, child-proof, Coca-Cola, co-op, co-worker, cut-throat

daddy-longlegs, daughter-in-law, deep-sea fishing, do-it-yourself, door-to-door, double-cross, double-dealing, double-park, Dow-Jones

ear-splitting, ex-husband, ex-serviceman, extra-territorial

face-saving, foot-and-mouth disease, forget-me-not, four-letter-word, fractions *(three-quarters, one-twentieth), fact-finding, father-in-law*

get-at-able, get-together, give-and-take, good-for-nothing, good-looking, grass-roots

habit-forming, half-and-half, half-breed (almost all words prefixed with *half-* carry a hyphen)*, hard-hat, helter-skelter, higgledy-piggledy, high-spirited, high-tech, hit-and-run, horse-racing, hand-picked, hand-me-down, hand-out, hands-off*

*ice-cream soda/cone (*but *ice cream), ill-advised, ill-timed, ill-treat, infra-red*

jack-o'-lantern, jiggery-pokery, Johnny-come-lately, jump-start

king-size, kiss-and-tell, knock-kneed, knock-for-knock

lady-in-waiting, Land-Rover, large-scale, Latter-day Saint, left-handed, light-headed, lily-white, long-distance runner/telephone call, loose-limbed, low-key

man-of-war, middle-aged, mother-in-law, mother-of-pearl, muu-muu

name-calling, near-sighted, ne'er-do-well, never-never, non-starter

O-level, off-peak, off-putting, old-fashioned, one-night-stand, out-of-doors

passer-by, penny-pinching, place-name, point-to-point, post-natal, pre-natal, price-fixing, pro-Irish, pro-life, etc, *punch-drunk*

quick-tempered, quick-witted, Queen-Anne (style)*, quick-change, quasi-legal*

re-cover (eg. a sofa)*, right-handed, right-minded, Rolls-Royce, rye-grass*

St Martin-in-the-Fields, Saint-Saens, sawn-off, set-aside, short-change, sister-in-law, son-in-law, sub-lieutenant, stick-up, sun-dried, swollen-headed

tax-free, test-tube baby, three-ring circus, tie-break, tip-off, T-shirt, trap-door spider, tutti-frutti, tut-tut, T-square, twin-tub, two-faced, two-sided

ultra-violet (but just as often *ultraviolet*), *U-turn, up-and-coming, ukiyo-e* (painting)

value-added tax, vice-presidential, V-day, V-J Day, voice-over

walk-on, walk-in, walkie-talkie, weather-beaten, weather-bound, well-known, well-thought-out, will-o'-the-wisp, warm-hearted, weak-willed, well-to-do, wedge-tailed eagle, well-read, well-informed, wide-awake, window-dressing, word-perfect, world-beater, worm-eaten, would-be, wych-elm

X-chromosome, X-ray (or x-ray)

Y-chromosome, yellow-belly, year-round, yo-heave-ho, yo-ho-ho

zero-rated

Punctuation: Symbols of Meaning

Apart from enabling us to join, separate and manipulate words and word units, punctuation also allows us to add extra meaning to bald statements:

You're going.	is not the same as	*You're going?*
Not again.	is not the same as	*Not again!*
Lucy and Joe's parents.	is not the same as	*Lucy's and Joe's parents.*
He said I'm mad.	is not the same as	*He said, 'I'm mad'.*

You can see that these marks possess the power to alter dramatically the meaning of statements – as it were with a single stroke. So learning how to use them, and how to use them correctly, is just as important as learning the functions of nouns and pronouns, adjectives and adverbs.

The Question Mark

The exclamation mark and question mark share a common ancestry. The exclamation mark consists of a hanging stroke pointing emphatically to the stop to make the reader screech to a halt. The **question mark** has a squiggle atop the stop, not unlike a 'q' (for *query*?), and its purpose is to warn the reader that the preceding word or statement is interrogative, or of doubtful validity.

A sentence that asks a question *directly* requires a question mark, but a sentence that poses an *indirect question* does not:

DIRECT QUESTION   *Are you going to the match?*

INDIRECT QUESTION *I asked him if he was going to the match.*

This looks fairly simple but sometimes an indirect question can be disguised:

> *Why should allegations that go unchallenged in America be the subject of legal action in Britain, asks Roy Greenslade.*

Not a question mark in sight. Now look at this similar example:

> *I wonder how many people will be homeless this Christmas?*

The first example seems to be shouting for a question mark after *Britain*, but if you study the sentence carefully you will see that it is just a novel form of an indirect question. We could rewrite it more clearly as an indirect question:

> *Roy Greenslade asks why should allegations that go unchallenged in America be the subject of legal action in Britain.*

Or, in the form of a reported direct question:

> *Roy Greenslade asks, 'Why should allegations that go*
> *unchallenged in America be the subject of legal action in*
> *Britain?'*

The second example is also an indirect question, so why is it followed by a question mark? This is because many writers fall into this error; the sentence should end with a full stop. Either that, or rewrite the sentence to include a direct question:

> *I wondered, 'How many people will be homeless this*
> *Christmas?'*

Generally question marks come at the end of sentences but sometimes can be inserted within them:

> *Perhaps – who knows? – there may in the future be some*
> *belated recognition for his services to mankind.*

Don't forget that, no matter how long your sentence is, if there is a direct question contained in it, the question mark is still required:

> *Is it not curious that 'Lourdes', which within a year of*
> *publication sold over 200,000 copies, had critical acclaim*
> *poured over it like champagne and which provoked such a*
> *furore that it was instantly placed on the Vatican's Index of*
> *prohibited books, is not still widely read today?*

The 'Semi'-question

One very common use of the direct question is in the form of a polite request:

*Would you let me know if either Monday or Tuesday next
week will be suitable?*

There is little doubt that the question mark is required; it is
after all a straightforward question directed at someone. But here's
a similar request-question:

*Would you be good enough to ensure that in future cars and
other vehicles belonging to non-staff are parked outside the
gates.*

Well, what is it – a request or a question? It is in fact both;
part question, part demand, and writer and reader both sense that
a question mark would weaken its authority. Many writers are
troubled by this weasel-like quality. Look at these examples – all
questions but all reasonably comfortable without a question mark:

*You're not going to give in yet, I trust.
I hope you're not calling me a liar.
I wonder if I might borrow the car tomorrow.*

In these cases, the expressions of personal feeling – *I trust*, *I
hope* and *I wonder* – tend to undermine the question content of the
statements. If you wrote *You're not going to give in yet*? or *May I
borrow the car tomorrow*? you'd unhesitatingly finish with question
marks. But there are some questions that look quite strange with a
question mark:

How dare you?   *How dare you!*

Here the expression is more an angry exclamation than a
query, and a question mark would, in most similar cases, seem
inappropriate.

186

The Exclamation Mark

Discouraged, if not banned, by modern newspapers (where it is referred to as a 'startler', 'gasper', 'screamer', and by tabloid sub-editors as a 'dog's dick'), and with a reputation for over-use, the **exclamation mark** nevertheless earns its keep with a surprisingly wide range of legitimate uses.

It's hard to imagine the following examples conveying anything like the same force and feeling without the screamers:

Shut up!   *You bitch!*   *What a mess!*   *Damn!*

Literature would undoubtedly be the poorer without them. Good writers aren't afraid of exclamation marks and use them judiciously for a number of functions:

CONVEYING ANGER, SCORN, DISGUST	*You're out of your mind!* *You must be joking!*
INDICATING SARCASM AND REVERSE MEANING	*Thanks a lot!* *That's bloody lovely, that is!*
UNDERLINING INSULTS AND EXPLETIVES	*You bastard!* *Shit!*
CONVEYING IRONIC TONE	*You're not so smart!* *And you said we wouldn't win!*
COMMANDING	*Come here! Right now!* *Get lost! And don't come back!*

All very well, but remember H W Fowler's warning: 'Excessive use of exclamation marks in expository prose is a certain indication of an unpractised writer or of one who wants to add a spurious dash of sensation to something unsensational'. Let this piece of gush provide a cautionary reminder:

*Patricia went to Venice – again! That's the second time in a
year!! And you'll never guess who she met there!!!*

The Apostrophe

Most of us have seen and chortled over everyday apostrophic
clangers like these:

Lilie's, Anemone's and Mum's (London florist's shop)
Fresh Asparagu's (Edinburgh greengrocer)
Her's is a warm, informal home. (newspaper interview)
Bargain Mens Shirt's (street market sign)
This school and it's playground will be closed over Easter
(sign on gate of a Croydon primary school).

If we're honest many of us have to admit that there are
times when we're forced to think quite hard about the use – or
non-use – of apostrophes. So what's the problem?

The problem lies simply in an ability to recognise that there
are two – and only two – kinds of apostrophes. One kind indicates
the possession of something; the other kind indicates a contraction
or abbreviation – a letter or letters left out of a word:

POSSESSIVE APOSTROPHE *Did you know **Jack's car** is a write-
off? I heard that **Jack's kids** have
the flu.*

CONTRACTION APOSTROPHE *Did you know that **Jack's** had a
bad accident? I heard that **Jack'll**
be out tomorrow.*

In the first two examples the apostrophes tell us that the car
and the kids belong to Jack; they are **possessive apostrophes**. In
the second pair of examples the apostrophes tell us that something
is left out: that *Jack's* is a shortened version of *Jack is*, and that

Jack'll is a shortened version of *Jack will*; they are **contraction apostrophes**. We're (*We are*) expected to work out what these mean, and with a little experience we soon learn to fill in the gaps:

> *My God! Did you hear? London's burning!* (contraction: *London **is** burning*)
> *I hope London's fire services can cope!* (possessive: *the fire services that belong to or are situated in London*).

Possessive Apostrophes

If we wish to indicate that something belongs to somebody we use the possessive apostrophe: *Joyce's house, Michael's mountain bike, the girl's tunic, his uncle's car, her grandfather's clock*.

Possession, ownership or association can also apply to things: *a good day's work, the company's policy, the tree's branches, the door's hinges*.

And the same goes for certain plural nouns: *men's trousers, children's toys, mice's tails, people's charter*.

No problems there. But all the above examples have something in common: none of the possessor words or names ends with an 's' – *Joyce, Michael, girl, uncle, grandfather, day, company, tree, door, men, children, mice, people*, etc. So what's the problem with words ending with an 's'?

The problem is that adding possessive apostrophes to words and names such as *boss, surplus, Thomas*, and to plurals such as *cats, hours* and *friends*, is not such a straightforward business. Let's look at some examples:

WORDS AND NAMES ENDING WITH 'S'	POSSESSIVE FORM
the boss	*the **boss's** temper*
Thomas	***Thomas's** recent illness*
mistress	*a **mistress's** secrets*
Charles Dickens	***Dickens's** novels*

Now see what happens when *plural nouns* that end with 's' become possessive:

PLURAL WORDS ENDING WITH 'S'	POSSESSIVE FORM
Penny's parents	*Penny's **parents'** caravan*
her friends	*her **friends'** parties*
the members	*the **members'** privileges*
our employees	*our **employees'** bonuses*
the girls	*the **girls'** classroom*

Get the picture? For singular ownership we simply add *'s,* but for plural or shared ownership we add the apostrophe *after* the *s – s'.* The system enables us to distinguish the different meanings. When we read:

*The opera star heard the **girl's** singing*

we are being told that the star listened to only one girl singing, whereas

*The opera star heard the **girls'** singing*

tells us (if we've learned the rules!) that the diva is listening to many girls singing.

In some cases, especially with names, we have choices, according to taste. We can add the final *'s* (*Tom Jones's songs, Prince Charles's opinions*) or drop it (*Wales' ruggedness, Dickens' characters, Jesus' teachings*), or observe tradition (*Queens' College, Cambridge; Queen's College, Oxford*).

However, beware of adjectives that look like possessives, such as ***games*** *mistress* which require no apostrophe. And watch out for units of time, such as *a **day's** work, a **minute's** delay* and *six* *months'* salary in complex sentences such as these:

> *I'm taking a three weeks holiday in three weeks' time.*
> *An hour's delay or two hours' delay – I wish the airline*
> *would tell us the facts.*

In the first example, the first *a three weeks* is an adjective phrase modifying the noun *holiday*. The second *three weeks'* has a possessive apostrophe to indicate that they are attached to the time that will elapse before the holiday is taken. In the second sentence both apostrophes are possessive: the first attached to the singular *hour = hour's*, and the second to the plural *hours = hours'*. Strictly according to the rules!

Pronouns can also be perplexing. Some have possessive apostrophes and some do not:

PRONOUNS WITH APOSTROPHES   *one's problems, anyone's idea, someone's shoes, one another's responsibilities, nobody's fault, anybody's luggage, each other's possessions*

PRONOUNS WITHOUT APOSTROPHES   *his, hers, its, ours, yours, theirs*

The most difficult apostrophe placements of all are probably those that serve to indicate a missing possession:

Sotheby's	stands for	*Sotheby's Auctions*
Lord's	stands for	*Lord's Cricket Ground*
Cruft's	stands for	*Cruft's Dog Show*

Confusion arises when such organisations drop the apostrophe. *Harrods, Ladbrokes, Womens Institute, Pears Soap. Lloyds Bank plc* carries no possessive apostrophe, but *Lloyd's* (standing for

Lloyd's coffee house, the place where the famous London insurance house began business in the 17th century) does. In this context you may care to ponder over this unusual example of apostrophe usage, from an article in *The Times* :

> *Sally Knowles, a name, said: 'When is Lloyd's going to accept that their's has been a society of overpaid incompetents and cunning, greedy people who make double-glazing and time-share salesmen look like amateurs?'*

These are unusually strong words but the most unusual word is *their's*. We have noted that *theirs* is a pronoun that never carries an apostrophe, so can this usage be correct? There is a fallacious notion that as the pronoun stands for *Lloyd's [Society of Underwriters]*, a 'double' possessive pronoun is required: *their's*. This is wrong, although similar forms of possessives are legitimate (*that story of Fred's* = Fred's story; *a friend of my father's* = my father's friend). If you find yourself not fully understanding the role of your apostrophe, reconstruct the sentence.

Contraction Apostrophes

One of the most frequent errors is the use of *it's* for the possessive form of *it*. This is wrong, of course: *it's* is the accepted contraction for *it is* or *it has*. For the record:

POSSESSION   *The newspaper claimed **its** punctuation record was unmatched by any of its rivals.*

CONTRACTION   ***It's** (It is) a fact that the punctuation record of the newspaper **isn't** (is not) so clever after all.*

Also for the record is this list of most of the accepted contractions:

aren't	*are not*	**she'll**	*she will, she shall*
can't	*cannot, can not*	**she's**	*she is, she has*
couldn't	*could not*	**there's**	*there is*
hasn't	*has not*	**they'll**	*they will, they shall*
haven't	*have not*	**they're**	*they are*
he'll	*he will, he shall*	**they've**	*they have*
he's	*he is, he has*	**we'll**	*we will, we shall*
I'd	*I would, I had*	**weren't**	*were not*
I'm	*I am*	**who's**	*who is, who has*
it's	*it is, it has*	**won't**	*will not*
I've	*I have*	**wouldn't**	*would not*
let's	*let us*	**you'll**	*you will, you shall*
ma'am	*madam*	**you're**	*you are*
mustn't	*must not*	**you've**	*you have*

There are many more idiomatic contractions: *sweet'n'lo*, *'alf a mo'*, *finger lickin'*, *Ah'm talkin' to yuh*, *rock'n'roll*, and so forth. Some antique contractions survive: *o'er* (over), *ne'er* (never) and *e'en* (even). But quite a few common words formerly carrying contraction apostrophes (*'cello*, *'flu*, *'phone*, *'til*, for *violoncello*, *influenza*, *telephone* and *until*) are now accepted without them.

One final apostrophic tip: *who's* is short for *who is* or *who has*; *whose* indicates possession: *whose wallet is this?*

Quotation Marks

Although **quotation marks** are often called 'inverted commas', if you look closely you will find they are not. You'll see that only the opening mark is inverted – that is, with the 'tail of the tadpole' pointing up; the closing mark is a normal raised or hanging comma or pair of commas. So we should use the term *quotation marks* (or *quotes* for short) exclusively.

Another thing about quotes that bothers some people is

whether to use single ('single') marks or double ('double') marks:

> *Heather said flatly, 'I never want to see him again.'*
> *Heather said flatly, "I never want to see him again."*

Newspaper and book publishers are divided on this; while most use double quotes, many have switched to single quotes perhaps because they are less typographically fussy – it's a matter of taste. But whether you use double or single marks you need to be aware of the convention for enclosing a quoted passage within another. If you are a single-quote writer, an additional direct speech quote within your first quote must be enclosed within double marks (or vice versa):

> *The sales assistant said, 'We only have them in grey and blue*
> *but yesterday my boss told me, "I don't know why they don't*
> *make them in other colours".'*

On the rare occasions where it is found necessary to have a third quote within a second quote in the same sentence, the formula is single/double/single, or double/single/double.

Quoting Direct Speech

When we read a newspaper report or story we want to know when we're reading reported or paraphrased speech and when we're reading words actually spoken. Quotation marks allow us to differentiate between the two forms:

> *Mr Murphy said that in his view the value of the pound*
> *would drop towards the end of the year. 'I also believe most*
> *European currencies will follow suit,' he added.*

This tells us that the writer has summarised the first part of the statement in his own words, and we have to accept that his summary is a correct interpretation of what Mr Murphy said. But we should have no doubts about the accuracy of the second part of the statement because the quote marks have signalled that the words are those actually spoken by Mr Murphy.

When you are quoting direct speech you must ensure that the words enclosed by your quotation marks are *exactly* those spoken. Not approximately, but *exactly*. Important – and costly – legal actions have been won and lost on this point.

It is also vital to make sure your reader knows who is responsible for the quoted statement. This is usually accomplished by what is called a *reporting clause*, which can introduce the statement or follow it or even interrupt it:

- ***Jones stated**, 'I am innocent and I can easily prove it.'*

- *'I am innocent and I can easily prove it,' **Jones stated**.*

- *'I am innocent,' **Jones stated**, 'and I can easily prove it.'*

Another point to remember is that when quoted speech is interrupted by a reporting clause, two rules apply. If the quoted statement is interrupted at the end of a sentence it should be finished with a comma and resumed with a capital letter:

> *'I knew I'd seen that bird before,' said Gavin. 'It was a cormorant, wasn't it?'*

But if the speech is interrupted mid-sentence, it should be resumed in lower-case:

> *'Don't you agree,' asked Gavin, 'that the bird over there is a cormorant?'*

How to Close Quotations

It is easy to remind writers not to forget to close their

quotation; like enclosing brackets, the marks always operate in pairs. What is a little more difficult is . . . *how?*

Look at this example:

Louis then asked her, 'Do you think I'm drunk'?

Do you place the question mark *outside* the quotation mark that closes the direct speech, or *inside*?

Louis then asked her, 'Do you think I'm drunk?'

The answer is that it depends on the relationship between the quotation and the sentence that contains it. The rule is worth engraving on the memory:

PUNCTUATION MARKS (full stops, commas, question and exclamation marks, etc.) GO **INSIDE** THE FINAL QUOTATION MARK IF THEY RELATE TO THE QUOTED WORDS, BUT **OUTSIDE** IF THEY RELATE TO THE WHOLE SENTENCE.

In our example, the question mark relates only to the quoted statement, *'Do you think I'm drunk?'* and so it rightly belongs *inside* the final quote mark, *not* outside.

But let's change the sentence slightly:

Should Louis have asked her, 'Do you think I'm drunk'?

Here, if you remember the rule, you can see that the question is an essential part of the whole sentence, and so the question mark *outside* the final quote mark is correct. To be pedantic, the sentence should properly be written like this:

Should Louis have asked her, 'Do you think I'm drunk?'?

Here you see that the quotation has its own question mark *inside* the final quote mark (quite correctly), and the overall sentence has its mark *outside* (again correctly). But the two piggybacked question marks look a bit silly and everyone accepts that in a case like this the inside question mark can be dropped without causing confusion.

With full stops, however, a different principle applies. If the quotation is a complete sentence that would normally end with a full stop, the stop *outside* the final quote marks is omitted and the whole sentence ended with a stop *inside* the final quote mark:

WRONG   *Louis tried to tell her, 'I think I'm drunk.'.*

CORRECT   *Louis tried to tell her, 'I think I'm drunk.'*

British and American Punctuation

With an increasing number of American-published and printed books circulating in Britain it is understandable that the aforegoing rules could cause confusion. They are, in fact, rules peculiar to British English. American English (and that of some Commonwealth countries) adopts a significantly different rule about quotation marks.

Generally, quotation marks in British English are logical in that they are placed according to sense and context. Their placement in American English may lack logic but does have the virtue of simplicity: *all punctuation* (stops, commas, colons and semicolons, exclamation and question marks, etc.) ***precedes*** *all final quotation marks*.

Compare the following examples:

ENGLISH QUOTE MARKS   AMERICAN QUOTE MARKS

Dr Johnson described a lexicographer   Dr Johnson described a lexicographer

as 'a harmless drudge'.	*as 'a harmless drudge.'*
Dr Johnson said that a lexicographer was 'a harmless drudge', yet was himself one.	*Dr Johnson said that a lexicographer was 'a harmless drudge,' yet was himself one.*
The lecturer said that 'Dr Johnson described a lexicographer as "a harmless drudge".'	*The lecturer said that 'Dr Johnson described a lexicographer as "a harmless drudge." '*

Most punctuation marks are multi-functional and quotation marks are no exception. They can be used to indicate titles (*His favourite film was the Marx Brothers' classic, 'Duck Soup'*); to identify nicknames (*Henry 'Rabbit Punch' Watson; Al 'Scarface' Capone*); to indicate doubt, cynicism or disbelief (*the hamburgers contained a mixture of liver, chicken parts and 'organic' beef*); and to indicate that a word or phrase should not be taken literally (*We are 'giving away' this nationally advertised Pyramid X100 Fresh Air Ioniser for only £19.99*).

The Three-dot Ellipsis

The science fiction pioneer H G Wells is credited with the invention of this mark . . . the **three-dot ellipsis**. But Mrs Henry Wood's immortal line, 'Dead! and . . . never called me mother', from the stage version of *East Lynne* (1874) antedates Wells' claim by at least a couple of decades. What this line of dots does is to indicate missing matter, which may consist of a single word:

Get the . . . out of here!

or matter considered to be non-essential:

Yesterday the shares stood at just over £4.65 which if you believe last night's closing statement . . . at that price the company is valued at almost £1.6 billion.

or an implied quotation or phrase which the reader is expected to know:

> *So then she bought contact lenses: you know, men don't make passes . . . And she really believes that, too!*

or indicating an unfinished thought:

> *The troubling question was, would Mrs Benedict sue, or . . .*

or indicating a time lapse:

> *Kimball crashed to the floor with eye-wincing force . . . only later, much later, in the darkness, did he realise he was a marked man.*

or indicating disjointed speech:

> *She paced the room. 'I don't know . . . every way I look at it . . . what would you do?' She drew deeply on the cigarette. 'I mean, surely he wouldn't do this to me . . . or would he?'*

The Asterisk

This complaining letter to *The Times* adequately explains the function of the **asterisk**:

> *In your paper last week I noticed a f***, a b***** and a f***ing and this made me wonder just who you think comprises your readership. If you feel that you have to censor any word that could possibly upset anybody, why do we not have M****** H****tine, the M********t Treaty and the C****n Ag*********l P****y?**

The final asterisk is in its customary role of guiding the

reader to a footnote or explanation elsewhere in the text, thus:

> * *Michael Heseltine, Maastricht Treaty, Common Agricultural Policy.*

Bullets

In our busy age the **bullet point** (● in this text) has found increasing favour, perhaps because:

- It enables us to summarise clearly a series of facts or conclusions.

- It sends a signal to the eye that 'here are the essentials'.

- It encourages writers to be brief: to use words and phrases rather than long sentences.

- It captures readers who are too lazy or too harassed to read solid texts.

The Stroke

Fancily called the virgule, solidus, shilling mark, slash and diagonal, this oblique **stroke** has a few limited uses:

TO INDICATE OPTIONS	*It depends upon how he/she behaves. The situation calls for guile and/or force.*
TO SEPARATE LINES OF VERSE	*The mist as it rises / touched with gold of the morning / Veils over the sadness / and the spirit lifts, soaring . . .*

Italics, Bold and Underlining

As tools for separating, highlighting and clarifying text,

these devices are on the margins of punctuation. Although they can hardly apply to hand-written prose, in this word-processing age the *italic*, **bold** and <u>underline</u> keys make possible a range of typographic effects. They have all been used in this book:

FOR EMPHASIS	Do **not** use a capital letter after a colon.
TO DISTINGUISH A WORD OR WORD GROUP	Less than a century ago, <u>tomorrow</u> was hyphenated as <u>to-morrow</u>.
TO IDENTIFY EXTRACTS AND QUOTATIONS	*The Collins English Dictionary* describes an adjective as **a word imputing a characteristic to a word or pronoun.**
TO INDICATE TITLES	Several errors involving quotation marks will be found in Jane Austen's *Pride and Prejudice*.
TO INDICATE A FOREIGN WORD OR PHRASE	The movement's meetings were always heavy with *Sturm und Drang*, shouting and argument.

Capitalisation

Capital letters are a form of punctuation in that they help guide the eye and mind through a text. Try reading this:

on sunday, april 7, easter day, after having been at st paul's cathedral, i came to dr johnson, according to my usual custom. johnson and i supt at the crown and anchor tavern, in company with sir joshua reynolds, mr langton, mr [william] nairne, now one of the scotch judges, with the title of lord dunsinan, and my very worthy friend, sir william forbes, of pitsligo.

That's a paragraph shorn of capital letters. It's readable, with some effort, but how much easier would the eye glide through it were it guide-posted with capitals at the start of each sentence, name and the abbreviation *Mr*!

Capitals are used at the beginning of sentences, after full stops, and for the first word in direct speech:

CORRECT *Sentences begin with capitals. And they follow full stops.*

WRONG *They do not follow commas, Nor do they follow semicolons or colons; But they do follow exclamation and question marks.*

CORRECT *He told us, 'Always use a capital when quoting direct speech.'*

WRONG *He told us, 'always use a capital when quoting direct speech.'*

Using capital letters to start sentences and surnames is clear enough, but a good deal of mystery surrounds the use of capitals in some other areas of writing. Here is a brief **Guide to Capitalisation**:

Aircraft	*Concorde, Airbus, Boeing 747,* etc.
Armed Forces	*British Army, Italian Navy, Brazilian Air Force,* but *navy, air force*. Ranks are capitalised: *Sergeant, Admiral, Lieutenant,* etc.
The Calendar	*Monday, March, Good Friday, the Millennium Dome* but *the new millennium*.
Compass points	*north-west, south-south-west* but *mysterious East, deep South, frozen North*.
Days	*Christmas Day, New Year's Day, Derby Day*.

The Deity

God, Father, Almighty, Holy Ghost, Jesus Christ; also *Bible, New Testament, Book of Common Prayer, Koran, Talmud,* etc; and religious *(Judaism, Baptists, B'nai B'rith). Hades,* but *heaven and hell.*

Diplomatic

Nicaraguan embassy (embassy is lower case).

Dog Breeds

Labrador, Afghan hound, Scotch terrier etc, but *rottweiler, lurcher, bulldog,* etc. lower case (check the dictionary as capitalisation is inconsistent).

Exclamations

Oh! Ahrrgh! Wow!

First Person Pronoun

I told them that I was leaving.

Flora and Fauna

Arab horse, Shetland pony, Montague's harrier but *hen harrier* (caps where a proper name is involved). Plants are l.c. but with scientific names orders, classes, families and genuses are capitalised; species and varieties are l.c.: *Agaricus bisporus.*

Geographical

The West, the East, the Orient, Northern Hemisphere, Third World, British Commonwealth, the Gulf, the Midlands, South-East Asia.

Headlines

With cap and l.c. headlines, capitalise nouns, pronouns, verbs and words of four or more letters. Generally, capitalise *No, Not, Off, Out, So, Up* but not *a, and, as, at, but, by, for, if, in, of, on, the, to* except when they begin headlines. Capitalise both parts of hyphenated compounds: *Sit-In, Cease-Fire, Post-War.*

Heavenly Bodies	*Mars, Venus, Uranus, Ursa Major, Halley's Comet.*
History	*Cambrian Era, Middle Ages, Elizabethan, the Depression, Renaissance, Year of the Rat.*
Law and Lords	*Lord Chancellor, Black Rod, Master of the Rolls, Lord Privy Seal, Queen's Counsel.*
Local Government	*council,* but *Kent County Council, Enfield Borough Council, Lord Mayor of Manchester.*
Member of Parliament	lower case, except when abbreviated: *MP.*
Nations, Nationalities	*Venezuela, Alaska, Brits, Estonians, Sudanese. Indian ink, Indian file, Indian clubs,* but *indian summer; French polish, French stick, French kiss, French letter* but *french window; Chinese,* but *chinaware; Turkish bath, Turkish delight.*
Personification	*The family gods were* **Hope** *and* **Charity***.*
Political Parties,	*Tory, Conservative Party, Labour Party,*
Terms	*Liberal Democrats, Communist Party,* but *communist; Thatcherism, Leninist, Luddites, Marxist, Gaullist,* etc.
The Pope	*The Pope,* but *popes, Pope Paul, Pope John,* etc.
Proper Names	Names of people (*Tony Blair, Spice Girls*); places (*Europe, Mt Everest*); titles (*Pride and Prejudice, Nine O'Clock News*); epithets (*Iron Duke, Iron Lady*); nicknames (*Tubby Isaacs, 'Leadfoot' Evans*).
Races	*Aztecs, Shawnees, Aboriginals, Asiatics.*
Religion	*Rev Adam Black, Fr O'Brien, Sister Wendy, Mother Teresa, Archbishop of Canterbury, Catholics, Jew, Jewish, Semitic, anti-Semitism, Protestants.*

Royalty	*The Queen, Duke of Edinburgh, Prince of Wales, Queen Mother, Princess Anne, the Crown.*
Our Rulers	*Her Majesty's Government, House of Commons, Secretary of State, Chancellor of the Exchequer; Prime Minister* (*PM* when abbreviated).
Satirised References	*In Crowd, Heavy Brigade, She Who Must Be Obeyed, Bright Young Things, Her Indoors.*
Scouts	*Scouts, Guides, Cubs.*
Seasons	*spring, summer, autumn, winter* (all l.c.).
Street names	*road, avenue, crescent, square,* etc, but *Highfield Road, Spring Avenue, Eagle Crescent, Sloane Square,* etc.
Titles	*Sir Thomas More, Lord Asquith, Mr and Mrs, Dr,* etc.
Trade names, marks	*Hoover, Peugeot, Kentucky Fried Chicken, Gillette, Durex, Xerox,* etc.
Van	When writing Dutch names *van* is l.c. when part of the full name (*Hans van Meegeren, Vincent van Gogh*) but capitalised when used only with the surname (*Van Gogh, Van Dyke*).
von	In Germanic names, *von* is always l.c.
World War	Capitalise, as in *World War 1, World War 2.* The usage *first world war* or *second world war* is sometimes preferred.

Writing Good English:
THE ELEMENTS OF STYLE

Style is many things to many people. To *The Times*, 'style is the essence of good writing'. To Somerset Maugham, 'A good style should show no sign of effort. What is written should seem a happy accident.' To Matthew Arnold:

> *People think I can teach them style. What stuff it is. Have something to say and say it as clearly as you can. That is the only secret of style.*

It would be foolish to disagree with any of those views. But more to the point, style is the way in which writers use the language to express themselves. Take this excerpt from the poem *The Pelt of Wasps* by David Constantine:

> *The apples on the tree are full of wasps;*
> *Red apples, racing like hearts. The summer pushes*
> *Her tongue into the winter's throat.*

Those three lines evoke an autumnal mood with a combination of words that is unique to that writer. Except if we allow for the most bizarre coincidence, no other writer on earth, no matter how much he or she learns about grammar and style, will at any time now or in the future throw those words together in that particular way.

ELEMENTS OF STYLE

Just as certain blends of musical notes stir us deeply in some mysterious way, so certain combinations of words possess the strange power to freeze us in our tracks, to arouse us, inspire us, to echo in our minds for a lifetime. How is it done? Of course, everybody would like to know. For the present, though, we are earthbound. We have dutifully mastered the principles of English grammar and punctuation, some of us perhaps with the expectation of producing those fizzingly memorable passages that are quoted down the centuries as gems of Eng Lit. And indeed a few – perhaps *you* – will transcend the grammatical box of tricks to create real magical prose. For the rest of us, however, things aren't too bleak; at least we have the opportunity to learn to write good, crisp, clear English, which is no mean accomplishment.

But perhaps we can aspire to do a little more than that. An eminent stylist, the novelist and playwright Keith Waterhouse, insists that good English, even at its most utilitarian, should *sing*. He noted that although there have been great blind writers, from Homer and Milton and beyond, there have been no great deaf ones in the sense of 'being unable to hear one's composition in one's head, as Beethoven heard his music.' Waterhouse asserts that while the mind dictates what is to be written, the ear monitors what is going down on paper – or at least it should. Writers with a tin ear are never likely to write with precision, brevity and elegance – or with style. The following notes will not teach you to make your words sing. But they may help you towards that goal by encouraging you to look at the language with a spirit of adventure, to develop a critical ear, and to learn from writers who please and thrill us.

Remember the Basics

Achieving good writing is a learning process. Start out by writing simple, clear prose – no pyrotechnics, no words or expressions you don't quite understand – just tell it like it is.

Take Dr Samuel Johnson's advice, quoting what an old college tutor had told a pupil: 'Read over your compositions, and where ever you meet with a passage which you think is particularly fine, strike it out.'

Plain writing need not be dull writing. On the contrary, a good writer always keeps the reader foremost in mind, thinking constantly: 'Will I attract someone to read this? And if so, will readers grasp what I'm writing? Will they enjoy reading it . . . will they laugh at this joke . . . will they learn something?' If a warning bell rings, a good writer will unhesitatingly change words, switch phrases and sentences around, rewrite, revise and rewrite again . . . and again. It sounds like hard work but the end product is worth it and can produce enjoyment and satisfaction.

One of the masters of plain English, George Orwell, left us with half a dozen typically idiosyncratic but elementary rules for good writing:

1. Never use a METAPHOR, simile or other figure of speech which you are used to seeing in print.

2. Never use a long word where a SHORT WORD will do.

3. If it is possible to cut out a word, always cut it out.

4. Never use the passive where you can use the ACTIVE.

5. Never use a FOREIGN PHRASE, a scientific word or a JARGON word if you can think of an everyday English equivalent.

6. Break any of these rules sooner than say anything outright barbarous.

Build on Brevity

The Americans Strunk and White, in their 20 million-copy bestseller *The Elements of Style*, distilled an essay on the beauty of brevity into one paragraph:

> *Vigorous writing is concise. A sentence should contain no unnecessary words, a paragraph no unnecessary sentences, for the same reason that a drawing should have no unnecessary lines and a machine no unnecessary parts. This requires not that the writer make all his sentences short, or that he avoid all detail and treat his subjects only in outline, but that every word tell.*

Brevity here does not mean the extreme terseness of telegramese. That can rebound, as a showbiz reporter once discovered when he wired the actor Cary Grant, then in his sixties: 'How old Cary Grant?' The actor replied, 'Old Cary Grant fine.'

Few people these days want to write more words than necessary, or to be forced to read two hundred words when the information could have been conveyed in a hundred. But despite this, too many writers ignore the old saw, 'If you don't know when to stop, don't start.'

In the chapter *Let's Look at Sentences* (page 25) we saw how, by combining simple sentences into compound sentences, we can economise on words and even enhance clarity. It also demonstrated how to trim away 'sentence fat' using the grammatical device called *ellipsis*, something we learn to do mechanically.

A good writer will take the process further. Rather than spoonfeed the reader with every stodgy fact and prose with every 'i' dotted and every 't' crossed, a good writer will provide just the essentials – but presented in a way calculated to stimulate and engage the reader's intellectual participation.

Consider the following passage:

> *Garth burst into the rush-lit hut, flushed and breathless. 'Imogen is missing.' he gasped. His brother, Alfred, sprang up from his seat by the fire. Imogen, his and Garth's sister, had been acting strangely these past weeks. There were rumours that she'd been seen with someone who had been visiting the village recently. The brothers wondered if there was some connection between this person and Imogen's absence. They felt they should look for her, and Alfred picked up his sword. 'Let's go and find our sister,' he said.*

The prose style is simple and gives us a reasonably clear picture of what is happening. But wouldn't you agree that it is all a bit . . . well, pedestrian? Now let's see what a little surgery will do.

> *Garth burst into the rush-lit hut, flushed and breathless.*
> *'Imogen's gone!' he gasped. Alfred sprang from his seat by the*
> *fire. Their sister had been acting oddly these past weeks. A*
> *handsome stranger had been seen lurking around the village.*
> *Alfred grabbed his sword and shouted to his brother: 'Where*
> *is the bastard?'*

The word pictures painted in both passages are substantially the same: the dimly-lit hut, the missing sister, the two agitated brothers. But where in the first passage the writer is laboriously working through the scene and dropping heavy-handed hints about what has happened to Imogen, in the second the reader is provided with the clues and invited to *think* about what may have happened to Imogen. Quite obviously a reader confronted with the second passage is far more engaged in the action.

In his analysis of how we acquire and use language the American psychologist Professor Steven Pinker describes our propensity to write what he calls 'garden path sentences' consisting of two parallel thoughts that although stitched together in grammatically correct fashion, virtually defy understanding. Two examples:

> *The cotton that sheets are usually made of grows in Egypt, but*
> *the cotton clothing is usually made of grows in Mississippi.*

> *Carbohydrates that people eat are quickly broken down, but*
> *fat people eat accumulates.*

The description, 'garden path sentences' is apt because they take the reader on a ramble to a point where, well before the path ends, and with no signposts in sight, he is utterly lost. In these examples ellipsis – dropping the word *that* – has led the writer into an impenetrable fog. Critical re-reading and revision would have uncovered the errors.

The Quality of Life

Writing can be flat and dead or bursting with life and energy. Which do you think would be the easiest, most interesting and most enjoyable to read?

There are two generally acknowledged ways to breathe life into otherwise sound writing. One is to avoid abstract words and expressions, and the other is to use the active, rather than the passive, voice.

Avoid the Abstract. In the section on *nouns* we found there are several types, including *concrete nouns* and *abstract nouns*. A concrete noun is something perceptible, tangible – something you can touch and see and smell: *wood, table, hair, blood*. An abstract noun refers to ideas, concepts, qualities, states of mind: *beauty, fascism, doubt, truth, fear*. Because they represent nothing of substance, abstract nouns, adverbial and adjectival phrases make the reader's mind work harder. Concrete nouns, on the other hand, offer few difficulties and readers relate to them instantly.

There is nothing wrong with abstract words themselves – they all mean something and we couldn't do without them – but unfortunately we very easily fall into the trap of using them carelessly. If you find that your writing is becoming swollen with abstract words such as *amenity, aspect, basis, capability, cessation, element, factor, participation, situation*, etc, you will almost always find that, on re-reading, it is tortuous and unnecessarily difficult to follow and understand.

Change up to Active. Would you rather do something, or have something done to you? With the first choice, you are in control; with the second you are the subject of somebody's whim. That's about the difference between the *active voice* and the *passive voice*.

In the chapter *Let's Look at Sentences* (page 25), examples of both voices were compared and it wasn't too difficult to decide that the active sentences were more direct, lively and interesting than the passive sentences, which were a bit like ancient history.

But don't get too carried away by the notion that the active voice will always make your writing clear and dynamic. It depends. Try writing a description of how to tie a granny knot, or how to replace a drive belt on a vacuum cleaner. It is quite likely that an active voice construction will prove less enlightening than one rendered in the passive voice. Steven Pinker gives a good example of this:

ACTIVE *Reverse the clamp that the stainless steel hex-head bolt extending upward from the seatpost yoke holds in place.*

PASSIVE *Reverse the clamp that is held in place by the stainless steel hex-head bolt extending upward from the seatpost yolk.*

The passive voice is often the best choice when long, complex phrases are inserted into a sentence. However don't make the mistake of switching voices in the same sentence or paragraph; the results can lead to much head-scratching. Here is a pair of Pinker examples:

PASSIVE INTO ACTIVE *Some astonishing questions about the nature of the universe have been raised by scientists studying the nature of black holes in space. The collapse of a dead star into a point perhaps no larger than a marble creates a black hole.*

PASSIVE THROUGHOUT *Some astonishing questions about the nature of the universe have been raised by scientists studying the nature of black holes in space. A black hole is created by the collapse of a dead star into a point perhaps no larger than a marble.*

The lesson to be learnt here is that thoughts and sentences must be related to one another so as to help, not hinder, the reader. In the first example, the reader is confronted by the reference to black holes at the end of the sentence. 'What are black holes?' he is probably asking, so the writer obliges. However the sentence containing the explanation begins with another thought altogether (*The collapse of a dead star . . .*) and the reader is momentarily confused. By rendering the following sentence in the passive voice, the explanation of what black holes are can sit right next to the initial mention of them; the reader's curiosity is satisfied immediately.

But apart from such special cases you will find that the active voice, because it uses live and kicking verbs and generally results in shorter, sharper sentences, possesses a presence lacking in the passive. Writing consistently in the passive voice is a bit like living in the past, and can have a deadening effect on the reader. So it pays to develop an awareness of the two voices, and when to use them appropriately. If in your reading you come across a passage that pleases or impresses you, take a few seconds to analyse the writer's use of voice.

Direct Speech. One further way to infuse life into prose in certain circumstances is to relate what people have said in direct speech. This is something you might hesitate to do in personal or business letters, but which would be appropriate, and even refreshing, in many kinds of fiction and non-fiction writing.

Take this descriptive passage, for example:

> *I was surprised to hear that my wife's Uncle Ted and Auntie Gwen were getting divorced. They are both in their late 80s and only last year celebrated their 60th wedding anniversary. Apparently one of their problems was to convince the divorce court that they really did wish to get divorced and, if so, on what grounds, after all this time together. I heard that when*

*asked this, Auntie Gwen told the judge that she'd had quite
enough of married life with Uncle Ted.*

It's an interesting story, but the way it's told leaves the
reader a bit flat. Uncle Ted and especially Auntie Gwen must be, in
these unusual circumstances, a couple of real characters, but this
isn't conveyed at all. And the ending is lame, leaving the reader
with a sense of being cheated of a good punchline.

Without changing the facts of the account, why not replay
the court scene in your head, imagining the characters involved
and *hearing* what they are saying – or might be saying. Put this
down on paper and see what a difference it makes:

> *I was surprised to hear that my wife's Uncle Ted and Auntie
> Gwen were getting divorced. But apparently they faced some
> problems trying to convince the divorce court that they really
> did wish to split up for good. The judge could hardly believe it.
> 'How old are you?' she asked Auntie Gwen.
> 'I'm eighty-six,' she told the judge, who then asked Uncle Ted
> to state his age.
> 'Eighty-eight,' said Uncle Ted.
> 'And how long have you been married?'
> 'Sixty-one years,' Auntie Gwen told her.
> 'Sixty-one years!' said the judge in disbelief. 'And after all this
> time you want to get divorced?'
> I'm told that Auntie Gwen turned to the judge and said,
> 'Look, enough is enough.'*

Add Colour to your Word Palette

Are you vaguely conscious that you may be writing in
monochrome? Without the vibrancy, the variety, the sensuality and
fun of colour? Then what you need is a paint-box of verbal effects,
a word palette of literary devices called figures of speech:
metaphor, **simile**, **hyperbole** and **alliteration** and **wordplay**.

Metaphor. We're surrounded by everyday metaphors: *raining cats and dogs*, *mouth of the river*, *stony silence*, *he sailed into him*, *over the moon* . . . thousands of them are irrevocably part of the language. The difficulty is in inventing new ones, and those writers who can, and can inject them at appropriate places into their texts, are a step ahead of the rest of us.

The beauty of metaphor is that it has the ability to bring a dull expression vividly to life, and to explain a difficult concept with startling clarity. We still use Dickens's 'the law is an ass' probably because nobody else has come up with a better pithy description for the odd and illogical decisions that can issue from our law courts.

As you can see, metaphor is describing something by using an analogy with something quite different. If we read or hear that a person has 'egg on his face' we are expected to know that he wasn't the victim of a phantom egg-thrower, but has been left in a very embarrassing situation. Egg and embarrassment are connected only by a *wild flight of imagination* (metaphor *and* cliché!).

By all means invent new metaphors but try to avoid creaky old ones that have, through overuse, become clichés: *different kettle of fish, can of worms, level playing field, human guinea pigs, go by the board, fly in the ointment*. And in particular watch out for **mixed metaphors** such as *they were treading in uncharted waters, to better face the abyss of the future let us march forward together*, and *I smell a rat but I'll nip him in the bud*.

Simile. A simile makes a direct comparison between two dissimilar entities: *as fit as a fiddle, as good as gold, as sick as a parrot, he's crazy like a fox, ears like jug handles*. You'll note that invariably similes are introduced by the conjunction *as* or the preposition *like*.

The judicious insertion of a simile can enliven a piece of writing but will carry more force if it is timely and original. But, as with metaphors, creating apt similes is a special art. If your skill is on a par with Robert Burns (*My love is like a red, red rose*), Wordsworth (*I wandered lonely as a cloud*) or Cecil Day Lewis (*a girl who stands like a questioning iris by the waterside*), or an anonymous Aussie (*she was all over me like a rash*) then have fun with similes. Most of us, though, need to employ tired simile avoidance techniques to prevent our writing being clogged by such *hoary chestnuts* (a hoary chestnut itself!) *as sharp as a razor, dull as ditchwater, as pleased as Punch, as plain as a pikestaff,* and *as mad as a March hare.*

Hyperbole. Hyperbole is deliberate overstatement: wild exaggeration used to make an emphatic point. Someone who complains that *I'm dying of hunger, I could eat a horse* or *I could murder a good steak* would probably be perfectly satisfied with a hamburger. A person who offers you a *thousand apologies* would be somewhat taken aback if you insisted on having them.

As with other figures of speech, hyperbole has to be witty or courageous to succeed. It's a stylistic area that leaves us envious of the writers who coined such hyperbolic classics as *I got legless last night; couldn't fight his way out of a paper bag; couldn't organise a piss-up in a brewery* and *a diamond that would choke a horse.*

Alliteration and Wordplay. Making mischief with words is a way of having fun with the language and it's something every writer feels the urge to do at some point. However, intruding drollery into prose can fall *as flat as a pancake* (simile, cliché) if it isn't *up to scratch* (cliché), and even when it is it should be used sparingly.

Here are some of the more pastel shades you can squeeze on to your word palette:

Alliteration. Sing a Song of Sixpence and *Peter Piper picked a peck of pickled peppers* are examples of alliteration from the nursery – the repetition of stressed sounds in words adjacent to or near one another. Here's another example, in verse form, from the Gilbert and Sullivan opera, *The Mikado: To sit in solemn silence in a dull, dark dock / In a pestilential prison, with a life-long lock / Awaiting the sensation of a short, sharp shock / From a cheap and chippy chopper on a big, black block!* The alliterative-happy headlines of today's tabloids came a century later: *WHO TOLD THE CHOPPER WHOPPER? LEGGY LOVELY LANDS UP LEGLESS.*

Alliteration that's been clumsily shoe-horned into your writing will *stick out like a sore thumb* (simile, cliché) so don't strive for alliterative effect. Mellifluous alliteration involving at most two or three words in a sentence will, with the least assistance from you, often occur naturally if your writing is flowing well.

Colloquialism and Idiom. Knowing when and where to use colloquial, idiomatic and slang expressions is a matter of intention and experience. Their occasional use can certainly take the stuffiness out of some writing. We're talking here of such expressions as *get cracking, don't drop your bundle, go for it, give us a break, it'll be all right on the night, d.i.y.* (colloquialisms); *part and parcel, keep a straight face, pass the buck, how's tricks?, odds and ends* (idioms); *bimbo, ankle-biter, sprog, muttonhead, ballbreaker, jollies, tosser* (slang).

Litotes. (*pron.* **ly**-*toe*-***tees***) Litotes is understatement, the opposite of hyperbole. Some examples: *this is no easy task, he was not a little upset, it's not uncommon, she's not a bad writer.* In other words litotes is a way of asserting a statement by denying its opposite: *not bad* means 'good, fine, okay'. Litotes can convey fine shades of meaning, but use the device carefully; it can go off in your hand.

Synecdoche. This is a figurative device in which a part is substituted for the whole, or the whole for a part. Some examples: *We sent over 200 head to market yesterday* (meaning: We sent over 200 cattle to market); *For the armada the king assembled a fleet of some 600 sail* (meaning: a fleet of some 600 ships). Here the expressions use part of the cow and part of a ship to indicate the whole. Compare *England beat Australia by three wickets* (here the whole – *England* and *Australia* – is used to indicate part – the English and Australian cricket teams). The device is useful to achieve brevity and avoid repetition. One of the most common – and contentious – synecdochic expressions is *man*, which, in the sense of *mankind*, is only part of a whole – man *and* woman.

Puns and Humour. Attempts at humour can be the downfall of the adventurous but incautious writer. Perhaps that's why there are very few writers able to make their readers laugh. Although newspapers and magazines will pay the earth for them they still remain only a handful internationally. Are you likely to be one of them?

This is not to say that your writing should be uniformly po-faced. A lightness of touch is appreciated by any reader and it is no bad thing to aim at being amusing from time to time. A well-placed witty turn of phrase, a funny but apt quotation, a waggish allusion or mischievous irony – all these are within reach of writers prepared to be hypercritical of their work.

Outside of national tabloid headlines puns are regarded by many writers with deep suspicion. You could say that the national press just about owns this venerable literary form. The Duke of York puts on weight and becomes a headline: *THE DUKE OF PORK*; a well-known actress appearing in the panto Cinderella loses a couple of stone to be renamed *THINDERELLA*. A story about rare frogs being run over by motorists is headlined *HALT! MAJOR TOAD AHEAD*. Another story, about Royal thrift, puns on the children's song: *THEY'RE GUARDING THE CHANGE AT BUCKINGHAM PALACE*. In the stories themselves, a pun rate of one every five lines is not unusual.

However puns do sometimes transcend the 'Who was that piccolo I saw you with last night?' 'That was no piccolo. That was my fife.' standard. A *New York Post* theatre critic greeted a new play by American playwright Clifford Odets with the complaint, 'Odets, Where Is Thy Sting?' only to be outdone by the outspoken *New York Times'* Walter Kerr commenting on the Broadway opening of a dramatisation of Isherwood's *I Am A Camera* (later to become the musical *Cabaret*): 'I Am A Camera – Me No Leica.' If you can pun at that inspired level, the world will forgive you.

The Writer's Seven Deadly Sins

Acquiring a good writing style is as much about the avoidance of bad habits as the cultivation of sound practices. And bad habits do abound; few professional writers admit to being completely and consistently free of one writing sin or another. For sins they are in that they stand in the way of clear, concise, elegant writing. So here are seven, the *Writer's Seven Deadly Sins*: **circumlocution, tautology, gobbledegook, jargon, euphemism, clichés** and **overloading.**

Circumlocution. If you wish to avoid being accused of circumlocution, stick to the point! This is the sin of not expressing yourself directly.

If you intend to drive from London to Manchester in the most direct way you'd hardly wander off every motorway exit and then dither about on country lanes. The same principle applies to writing, and you'd be surprised how many people dither and wander, losing anyone trying to follow them in the process.

One sure sign of circumlocutory writing is the persistent use of certain long-winded phrases, most of which can be reduced to a single word. Here's a short list of the worst offenders, with suggested, direct substitutes:

apart from the fact that – *but, except*
as a consequence of – *because of*
at the time of writing – *now, at present*
at this moment / point in time – *now, at present*
avail ourselves of the privilege – *accept*
because of the fact that – *because*
could hardly be less propitious – *unpromising*
due to the fact that – *because*
few in number – *few*
I beg to differ – *I disagree*
in accordance with – *under*
in addition to which – *besides*
in a majority of cases – *usually*
in all probability – *probably*
in association with – *with*
in close proximity to – *near*
in connection with – *about*
in less than no time – *soon, quickly*
in more than one instance – *more than once*
in spite of the fact that – *although, even though*
in the light of the fact that – *because*
in the neighbourhood of – *near, about*
in the recent past – *recently*
irrespective of the fact that – *although*
notwithstanding the fact that – *even if*
of the opinion that – *think, believe*
on a temporary basis – *temporary, temporarily*
provide a contribution to – *help*
subsequent to – *after*
there can be little doubt that – *clearly*
until such time as – *until*
with a view to – *to*
with the exception of – *except*

Tautology. 'Mr and Mrs Smith are proud to announce the birth of a baby girl, Sarah Anne.' A fairly everyday announcement. But what if Mrs Smith had given birth to an *adult* girl? That would be newsworthy! The use of the word *baby* in the announcement is what is known as **pleonasm**, the use of redundant words. The same would apply if Mrs Smith had invited the neighbours in to see her 'new baby'. Are there any *old* babies? Here the word *new* is a pleonasm.

When a word repeats the meaning of another word in the same phrase it is called **tautology** and, usually, all verbal superfluities are known by this term. Avoiding redundant words and expressions is a sign of a caring writer and here, to help you, are a few of the more common transgressors.

actual facts
added extra / added bonus
advance warning
arid desert
audible click
collaborate together
consensus of opinion
couple together
each and every one
early beginnings
end result
final completion
forward planning
free gift
future prospects
gather together
important essentials
I saw it with my own eyes
joint / mutual cooperation

lonely isolation
merge together
necessary requisite
new invention
pair of twins
past history
personal friend
relic of the past
safe haven
totally complete / finished
quite / absolutely / utterly unique
unexpected surprise
usual habit
viable alternative

Gobbledegook. In 1944 a Texas congressman named Maury Maverick became so angry about the bloated bureaucratic language in memos he received that he described it as *gobbledegook*. Explaining the name he said it reminded him 'of an old turkey gobbler back in Texas that was always gobbledy-gobbling and strutting around with ludicrous pomposity. And at the end of this gobble-gobble-gobble was a sort of a gook.' Maverick was also the head of a federal agency, and promptly issued an order to all his subordinates: 'Be short and say what you are talking about. Let's stop *pointing up* programs, *finalizing* contracts. No more *levels*, *patterns*, *effectuating*, *dynamics*. Anyone using the words *activation* and *implementation* will be shot.'

Half a century later it seems that the Maverick Edict has had little effect. The sound of turkeys is ever-present. Here's a stunning sample from a Stanford University Press catalogue (1994) ironically touting a book about communication:

> *Converging with a leitmotiv in early deconstruction, with*
> *Foucauldian discourse analysis, and with certain tendencies*

> *in cultural studies, such investigations on the constitution of*
> *meaning include – under the concept 'materialities of*
> *communication' – any phenomena that contribute to the*
> *emergence of meaning without themselves belonging to this*
> *sphere: the human body and various media technologies, but*
> *also other situations and patterns of thinking that resist or*
> *obstruct meaning-constitution.*

That is a mental maze of gobbledook that, once entered, offers little chance of escape. One way to avoid lapsing into gobbledegook is to ask yourself three questions: *Do I fully understand what I'm writing about? Have I expressed in writing exactly what I want to say? Will **all** my readers understand what I'm saying?*

As with the other writers' sins, there are many signs that give the gobbledegookist away – pompous, meaningless phrases such as: *all things being equal, as of right now, in a manner of speaking, it goes without saying, of necessity, to all intents and purposes, within the foreseeable future.* Avoid them assiduously.

Jargon. Jargon consists of mostly unintelligible words and phrases, used either unthinkingly or to impress and appear smart and up-to-date.

But not all jargon is pretentious rubbish. It includes the shop talk of technical terms, understood by those who have to know and who have no need to explain them to outsiders. It is for millions of people a form of time-saving professional shorthand. It is a specialist's language designed for accurate and efficient communication between members of a particular group.

However, too often jargon and arcane verbiage are used by writers to trick others into believing they know more than they actually do; or exploited as a security blanket to give them the feeling of belonging to an elite. This use – or misuse – can only interfere with meaning and understanding. How many writers can hold hand to heart and say that they know *precisely* what these vogue words mean: *parameter, symbiosis, quantum leap, synergy, dichotomy, post-modern, deconstruction*? That such jargon is not understood properly doesn't stop a lot of writers from using it.

Some jargon even requires translation: *an unpremised business person* (street trader); *unselected roll-back to idle* (aircraft engine failure in mid-flight); *wilderness recreation* (camping and hiking); *festive embellishments* (Christmas lights). The job ads are full of jargon: *service-driven organisation, human resources, effective team-player, self-motivated, pivotal role, results-orientated, proactive, remit, product-specific marketing,* etc. A job ad for a health worker in Brazil announced:

> *You will assist the team in formulating and implementing a health policy, evaluating and developing appropriate responses to specific health problems in indigenous areas . . .*

If you eliminate the jargon from that passage you are likely to end up with plain English: *You will help to plan and carry out a policy to deal with health problems among local people.*

Here's a short list of jargon words and phrases that comply with the former US president Harry S Truman decree: 'If you can't convince 'em, confuse 'em'. Some jargon-free alternatives are shown.

accentuate – *stress*
accomplish – *do, finish, complete*
accountability – *responsibility*
axiomatic – *obvious*
bullish – *confident*
come on stream – *start working*
core – *basic*
end of the day – *in the end*
funded – *paid for*
generate – *make, produce*

hidden agenda – *hidden / disguised purpose*
implement – *fulfil, carry out*
inaugurate – *introduce, start*
input – avoid this altogether or use *ideas*
name of the game – *object*
ongoing – *continuing, continual, constant*
precondition – *condition*
put on the back burner – *postponed, delayed, suspended*
state of the art – *latest, newest*
take on board – *understand, comprehend, accept*
track record – *experience*
user-friendly – *easy to use*
viable alternative – *alternative, choice, option*

Euphemism. Euphemisms – words and phrases people use to avoid making a statement that is direct, clear and honest – are often used out of kindness when the direct expression might offend. For example a deaf person is often described as *hard of hearing* and a part-blind person as *partially-sighted*. Unfortunately in recent times such traditional and harmless euphemisms have been further blunted and replaced by such terms as *aurally* or *visually challenged*.

Have you ever admitted that you might have been, well, to put it frankly – drunk? How often have you heard someone honestly admit they were drunk? No, they might admit to having been *one over the eight, high-spirited, squiffy, happy, a bit merry, worse for wear, tired and emotional* or any one of several hundred other euphemisms for drunkenness, but not *drunk*.

Euphemism is particularly effective for disguising crime – especially the crimes we might commit ourselves. *Tax fiddling, meter feeding, fare dodging, joy riding* and *being economical with the truth* sound like laudable streetwise skills whereas they all amount to cheating and criminal activity.

Euphemism can also help make the unpalatable positively mouth-watering. Those people we used to know as insurance salesmen are now variously *financial advisers, investment consultants, financial field sales managers, fiscal analysts, savings strategists, liquidity planners, pensions counsellors* and *endowment executives.*

The fertile breeding ground for euphemism today undoubtedly lies in the quest for what is popularly known as political correctness, or PC. This movement quite commendably seeks to banish stigmatising and dehumanising terminology from our speech and writing. It has been successful in removing from our everyday language such thoughtless and hurtful terms as *nigger, coon, cripple* and *OAP.* And it has been especially successful righting the centuries-old imbalance between the sexes in the popular perception. The use of *man* generically as a suffix or prefix is discouraged in some quarters, and terms such as *chairman, salesman, manpower, one-man show, man in the street, man-made,* etc. now have their feminine or neutral equivalents.

What became known as the 'Language Gestapo', however, pushed a PC euphemism too far. Attempts to emasculate the Lord's Prayer, to denigrate traditions and heroes, to desanctify Christmas and generally debilitate the language have resulted in a backlash of resistance. The outcome of a recommendation to plumbers in a guidebook issued by the Water Research Association to cease using the terms *female joints, ballcocks* and *stopcocks* was that customers were charged one price for fitting a ballcock and double the amount for installing a euphemistic *float-operated valve.*

A bizarre example perhaps, but a warning to every aspiring writer. Cultivate a sensible and sensitive attitude towards people and institutions, whether minorities or majorities, but ***say what you mean!***

Clichés. Some people have the extraordinary ability to think, speak and write in clichés: 'Y'know, not to beat around the bush or

227

hedge my bet, this section is a must-read because it tells it like it
is, y'know, calls a spade a spade and in a nutshell leaves no stone
unturned to pull the rug from under those dog-eared old saws that
have run their course and had their day, called clichés.'

These are the people who've given the cliché a bad name.
We all use them, of course. Sometimes that familiar phrase can be
the neatest way of expressing yourself and most of us have a
quick-draw cliché vocabulary of a thousand or two. But how aware
are we of the irritation that the overuse of clichés can cause?

To use clichés when it's appropriate and to avoid them when
not, it helps to be able to recognise them. Give yourself this quick
test: how many of these tired hand-me-downs can you complete
with the missing word?

1   *A gift from the . . . .*
2   *He's a . . . . . . of society*
3   *It's not over till the . . . lady sings*
4   *Light at the end of the . . . .*
5   *A little learning is a . . . . thing*
6   *By the . . . . of your teeth*
7   *If you've got it, ... it*
8   *It falls between two . . . . . .*
9   *. . . . it like the plague*
10 *A sight for . . . . eyes*

[**Answers:** *1. gods; 2. pillar; 3. fat; 4. tunnel; 5. dangerous; 6. skin;*
7. flaunt; 8. stools; 9. avoid; 10. sore]

Many modern clichés are 'stock modifiers' – Darby and Joan
combinations of words that, often for no reason, are always seen
together. A person isn't moved; he or she is *visibly moved*; a person
isn't merely courteous, he or she is *unfailingly courteous*. These
parasitic intensifiers are really sly clichés and you should try to
avoid them: *overriding importance, woefully inadequate, far-reaching*

consequences, *no-holds-barred interview* and *increasingly apparent* are just a few examples.

If you make up your mind to guard against clichés creeping into your speech and writing you'll be surprised how easy it is to do without them and how much fresher your writing becomes as a result. So don't touch clichés even with a ten-foot pole.

Overloading. Our seventh and final sin is the curious human impulse to allow the moving finger to write, and write, and write . . . on and on. In short, to cram as much into a sentence as possible.

Overloaded sentences do not have to be 500 words long. Here's one from a national newspaper with an unremarkable 47 words – but it is still loaded well above the Plimsoll line of saturated facts:

> *A man living alone was approaching his house when he was attacked by seven armed robbers who forced him at gunpoint to open the front door of his secluded country cottage in Kent before leaving him so badly beaten that he is now afraid to return home.*

The main news points in this opening sentence seem to be: (a) a man was badly beaten by robbers in his secluded cottage in Kent; (b) he was beaten so badly that he is now afraid to return home, presumably from hospital. The additional facts – that he was approaching his house when the attack took place, that there were seven robbers, that they were armed, that they forced him at gunpoint to open the front door – can wait a moment. The vital principle in a story like this is to give the main facts first. And if you think there are just too many facts for a single sentence, distribute them in two or more sentences to construct a gripping, but clear, opening paragraph:

> *A man living alone in a secluded cottage in Kent was beaten*
> *so badly by robbers that he is afraid to go home. Seven armed*
> *men struck as he approached his house and forced him at*
> *gunpoint to open his front door.*

Even though we now have two sentences we've managed to save five words. More importantly, the reading task is easier and the meaning is clearer.

A common feature of many overlong, overweight sentences is the presence of non sequiturs. A non sequitur is a statement that has little or no relevance to what preceded it – resulting in a sentence that attempts to join the unjoinable: *The egg-and-spoon race was won by eight-year old Julia Jones whose parents taught her to sing and tap dance.* You might well ask, what does singing and tap dancing have to do with winning an egg-and-spoon race? That is a non sequitur. Non sequiturs are usually the result of a writer's hankering to accumulate information with a minimum of punctuation, but the inevitable result is overload and confusion.

To avoid the sin of overload, re-read and rewrite. Or as someone once said – although not about overlong sentences – divide, and conquer.

Two aspects of good writing remain to be discussed – problems that can arise as you move from the basics of the writer's craft to achieving a 'voice' of your own. The first of these arises from a writer's misguided efforts to avoid repeating a word in a sentence; the second from excessive admiration of another's prose.

Elegant Variation

In a review of a biography of Abraham Lincoln by the historian David Donald, the novelist Martin Amis wrote: 'Although Donald may be as methodical as Lincoln, he is his junior not least in literary talent. The prose is continually defaced by that scurviest of all graces, Elegant Variation. Here is but one example of Donald's futile ingenuity: "If the president seemed to support the Radicals in New York, in Washington he appeared to back the Conservatives."' Although many might think that Amis was being a bit picky, he was surely justified, in defending the principles of style, in criticising the author's too-obvious recourse to a 'strained synonym'; rather than repeat *seemed to support* the author substituted *appeared to back*. This practice, abhorred by stylists, was first identified by the grammarian H W Fowler, who scornfully called it 'Elegant Variation'.

Every writer can face the problem of dealing with identical words or phrases appearing in the same sentence or an adjoining one. In writing dialogue, for example, the word *said* is likely to be repeated endlessly at the risk of annoying the reader. The quick solution is to substitute near-synonyms: *uttered, replied, responded, answered, retorted, remarked, announced, added,* etc. If such substitutions are used judiciously and with restraint the reader will probably not realise what is going on; fluency and readability will not be impaired.

Fowler offered an example of a paragraph constructed almost entirely of 'elegant variations' in a report on the activities of the late Mother Teresa:

> *A few months ago **she** seemed near death. But **the world's most famous nun** continues her good work. Today **Mother Teresa** announced she is so moved by the plight of Romanian children she is going to do something about it. **The Nobel Peace prize winner** will open a mission in Bucharest to care for the children.*

The writer doubtless thought that the phrases describing Mother Teresa avoided the repetitious use of her name and the pronoun *she*, and also packed more information into the paragraph.

Perhaps, but a succession of paragraphs like this would more likely grate on the reader's nerves.

Running to the thesaurus or synonym dictionary for a replacement word can trap the rookie writer who will proceed merrily unaware of the smell left behind to be picked up by the fastidious reader. Considering a reconstruction of the sentence might be a better solution, or even allowing the repeated word to remain if it doesn't jar.

Plagiarism

In their pursuit of rapid progress some ambitious writers are led up the dodgy path of plagiarism – words, ideas, stories or texts copied from the work of other writers. Very few writers have the gall to copy a work in its entirety and claim it as their own, but it has been done. More common is the practice of 'borrowing' someone else's work without indicating that it is by the use of quotation marks, or crediting its source. This can lead to complaint and legal action and every year in Britain there is at least one serious – and sometimes costly – accusation of plagiarism.

As a cautionary tale, here is the case of two books, one a biography of the Empress Eugenie published in 1964 by Harold Kurtz, and the other about royal brides by the Princess Michael of Kent, published in 1986:

'The Empress Eugenie' *by* **Harold Kurtz**	*'Crowned in a Far Country'* *by* **Princess Michael of Kent**
All her life Eugenie placed very little importance on sex, not as something wicked, just unimportant and cheap. 'You mean,' she would say in	*All her life Eugenie placed very little importance on sex; not as something wicked, just unimportant and cheap. 'You mean,' she would say in*

tones of incredulity, 'that men are interested in nothing but that?' when her ladies were chatting about the infidelities of men.	*disbelief, 'that men are interested in nothing but that?' when her ladies were chatting about infidelities.*

Be warned about purloining prose! And if you have heard that there is no copyright in literary ideas, concepts, structure and titles, take care also, because if it can be proved that you are 'passing off' another's original work as your own you could find yourself at the wrong end of a lawsuit.

To sum up . . .

- Brevity is beautiful. So is simplicity. Short words, too. And short sentences.

- Prefer concrete words to abstract, the active voice to passive, a positive tone to negative.

- Keep sentences harmonious – in voice, tense and number.

- *Listen* to what you write.

- Remember that it is *your* job to attract and keep the reader's attention.

Index

WRITING GUIDES BY GRAHAM KING

Graham King's invaluable guides to good English break down the barriers that prevent so many articulate, intelligent people from communicating effectively, and increase your word power without boredom!

COLLINS GOOD GRAMMAR

Picking up a book on grammar takes courage, but the learner can take heart from the fact that many of the great writers, including Charlotte Bronte, were hopeless at grammar at school. This easy-to-use guide features:

- The thirteen gremlins of grammar, from apostrophes to verbs
- The point of sentence construction
- The writing of good English
- Cartoons by Hunt Emerson

COLLINS GOOD PUNCTUATION

Punctuation has been described as 'a courtesy designed to help readers understand a story without stumbling'. Included in this essential guide are:

- A Victorian schoolmistress's 10 Golden Rules of Punctuation
- How to deal with capitalisation, full stops and commas
- Mastery of colons, parentheses, dashes, hyphen hassle, questions, exclamations and apostrophes
- The ultimate punctuation test
- Cartoons by Hunt Emerson

COLLINS GOOD WRITING SKILLS

The basic principle of this incredibly useful book is that 'clarity begins at home': say what you mean and you stand a better chance of getting what you want!

- How to write clearly, and what sort of language to avoid
- How to express what you really feel in letters
- How to create the perfect CV
- Cartoons by Hunt Emerson